A Woman of Steel

A VE Day celebration street party in Darnall, May 1945

Published by ACM Retro Ltd,
The Grange,
Church Street,
Dronfield,
Sheffield S18 1QB.

Visit ACM Retro at:
www.acmretro.com

A catalogue record for this book is available from the British Library.

Cover shot: Ruby Gascoigne (front row, far right) and colleagues from W. T. Flather's Standard Steel Works in World War Two

A Woman of Steel

Ruby - A Diamond Forever, The Sparkle In The Family Jewels

An air raid shelter in Chinley Street, Darnall

Stephen Johnson

The Staniforth Road/Main Road junction in the 1950s

The Lyric Picture House, Main Road, Darnall, in the 1970s

Foreword   6

Preface   7

Early Life   9

From Shop to Kitchen   16

Family & Friends   24

What With One Thing & Another   39

Unwanted News   52

High Days & Holidays   58

Women Of Steel   64

Crowning Glory   72

Statue   76

Final Thoughts   79

Bibliography   80

FOREWORD

I am delighted to have been asked to write the foreword for this biography of Ruby Gascoigne, one of Sheffield's Women of Steel. Ruby's story is similar to that of many Sheffield women of her generation. Reading it is fascinating but it also brings home the very vital contribution women made to keeping this country going during the Second World War.

The Women of Steel worked long and gruelling shifts doing hard and sometimes back breaking work whilst often, like Ruby, enduring wartime hardships and having to look after their families as well.

It is important that the story of Ruby and other Women of Steel is recorded and recognised to ensure that we and future generations understand more about their courage, determination and hard work at such a critical time in the history of this country.

Councillor Sylvia Dunkley
Lord Mayor of Sheffield

W T Flather's Standard Steel Works, Sheffield Road, Tinsley.
Sheffield Road runs left to right towards Sheffield

PREFACE

Most women in their eighties will be enjoying the twilight of their years. They've brought up their families and seen their grandchildren grow up, their great grandchildren, and maybe seen their great great grandchildren come along. Their working life will be long behind them. In the twenty, or perhaps thirty, years of retirement, they've become used to a more relaxed routine. A few may be of the adventurous kind, taking round the world cruises, enjoying exotic breaks and holidays. Some plucky ones may take the plunge and do a bungee jump or go sky diving. But not many would expect a whole new adventure to present itself and thrust them into the limelight.

This though is just what has happened to Ruby Gascoigne, who's clearly not one to let the grass grow under her feet. A letter to Sheffield's newspaper The Star by Kathleen Roberts, asking why the women of Sheffield who filled the places in the steel works left by the men who were called up for active service during the Second World War have never been formally recognised, led Ruby into a new and unexpected chapter in her life. From a quiet home life surrounded by her extensive family, Ruby has been interviewed on radio and television, been a guest speaker at lectures, had lunch at the House of Commons, been an inspiration for a book and a play, attended a Buckingham Palace Garden Party, and is now the subject of a biography. But whilst this book may not rank among the greatest biographies of all time, it is a portrayal of Ruby's life, and a snapshot of her fondest and saddest memories, of the things she holds dear, and the bits and pieces of modern life that cause her amazement and annoyance.

Ruby Gascoigne's life may be no different to that of any other ordinary woman of her age from a working class background in an industrial city like Sheffield. Born in the industrial east end of Sheffield she has known poverty. She had a happy childhood and was not afraid to start work. But nothing prepared her for her conscription into the steel works in the Second World War. She has known the bitterness, the harshness and the consequences of a devastating world war. She has coped with her own illnesses, and the sudden deaths of loved ones. In short she has coped with the ups and downs that life has thrown at her. An ordinary woman? She is no *ordinary* ordinary woman. And now a new lease of life has rejuvenated her and shown that she still has plenty to offer the modern world – and a few things to tell it!

Though principally about Ruby and her life, this book also serves to show the vast differences in lifestyles and attitudes between the time when Ruby was a young girl and young mother in the 1930s and '40s, and what people take quite for granted these days. At the same time it tells how what are now everyday items made their wondrous appearances in her lifetime, and how her family were pioneers in absorbing them into their homes.

Several sources have been used in the preparation of this book, principally Ruby herself. But the author would also like to thank the members of Ruby's family who have given their advice and their own invaluable contributions. Thanks go also to Sheffield Libraries, Archives & Information Services for permission to use images from the Picture Sheffield collection.

Stephen Johnson

EARLY LIFE

Ruby Gascoigne was born at home, 14 Uttley Street, Darnall, Sheffield, on Monday 18th September 1922, the daughter of Ben Hough and his wife Lavinia (neé Derby). Her parents had lived in the same yard when they were children. Her father had been a regular soldier and was now on the Army Reserve List. Her mother was a committed member of the Salvation Army. Ruby got on very well with her parents, especially her father, and the two remained very close. In the First World War her father served with the army in France and India, and was a proud member of the Home Guard in the Second World War.

On the day Ruby was born the Yorkshire Telegraph & Star, forerunner of The Star, was reporting on the so called 'Sheffield Chinese Mystery', the murder of Sing Lee, owner of a Chinese laundry at Crookes, a crime for which his assistant Lee Doon would later hang. It was also reported that George Mooney, head of the infamous Mooney Gang which roamed Sheffield streets in the 1920s, was fined 40 shillings for using offensive language in the street.

"Sheffield United's Poor Shooting" was costing them the game in that afternoon's match at Blackburn Rovers, they lost 0-1, but Yorkshire County Cricket Club, the then county champions, were doing well against a Rest of England Eleven at The Oval.

The London, Midland & Scottish Railway was offering return trips from Sheffield to the Carnival Week at Morecambe, whilst Dr Cassell's Tablets at 3 shillings a bottle would cure heart flutter, dyspepsia, nerve problems, amnesia, sleeplessness...

There was no shortage of relatives in the area where Ruby lived. Close by lived her mother's sister, Aunty Beatty, and often she would be at her house playing with her cousins Leslie, Derek, Margaret and Pearl. Ruby was somewhat protected at home, but playing with her cousins was her big chance to get dirty, though it meant a good scrubbing when she got home. Ruby was very fond of her Aunty Beatty, and she in turn would become very fond of Ruby's children, especially her eldest child Graham, whom she would take on trips to Cleethorpes whilst Ruby was doing her vital war work. When she was three years old Ruby's family moved to a new home on Fairfax Road, off the newly built Prince of Wales Road.

Ruby recalls that in her childhood people, especially housewives, were very house proud, and this despite the lack of amenities that would today render a house uninhabitable. The toilet was outside, there was no indoor bath, and the kitchen had a sink with one cold water tap. Hot water had to be provided by heating it in a coal fired boiler. Monday was wash day, which meant the boiler being lit for hot water, and the washing done by hand with a dolly, before being transferred to a hand operated wringer, or mangle, and then hung out in the yard to dry in the soot filled air. The traditional Monday meal was boiled potatoes with leftovers from the Sunday roast lunch. On Fridays the boiler was lit again ready to fill the tin bath that was brought in from outside and positioned in front of the fire. Starting with father then mother, one by one everybody would have a bath and then put on clean linen underwear that would last them through the next week. Steps were donkey stoned or shined with Red Cardinal, brasses and stair rods were polished, and the Yorkshire range black leaded when required. In Ruby's home her mother baked every week and the house smelled of fresh baked bread. No bought bread in the Hough household!

School life was no different to most other children's. At the age of five she went to her first school, Prince Edward's at the top of Prince of Wales Road. At the age of nine she went to Stand House Council School, and later to Pipworth Road Council School where in 1933 she took her 11+ exam. Ruby was very happy at Pipworth School and was keen on sports such as rounders and netball. She was a member of the school's teams that visited different schools playing in matches. From there she went to the Pupil Teacher Centre on Holly Street, next to Sheffield City Hall. The Centre and other buildings in this complex, including the former Firth College and the Central Technical Schools, later became the offices of the Sheffield Education Committee. They now comprise the Leopold Hotel and several restaurants.

Whilst at the Pupil Teacher Centre Ruby's health suffered. There were episodes of scarlet fever and diphtheria, not uncommon in 1930s Sheffield, and rheumatic fever, and three months of school were lost. Despite this she was able to take advantage of some additional tuition to help her catch up. She had help with her homework from her father, and her favourite subjects were maths and English, but algebra was the cause of a near nervous breakdown. More school time lost meant that a prospective career in teaching was cut short and Ruby left school at fifteen. Ruby's links with her childhood have continued through her lifelong friendship with two school friends who maintained close contact for the last seventy odd years.

In the 1920s and '30s when Ruby was growing up, unemployment and poverty was rife. Even living in Darnall, on the doorstep of such major firms as Hadfields and Edgar Allen's, was no guarantee of work for the men. The economic depression of the era had led to closures of all sorts of firms with men thrown out of work in their thousands. In those days there was no unemployment benefit (Jobseeker's Allowance as it is called today) and only limited state relief. But this was means tested and people would be expected to sell their furniture before any relief would be paid. Furthermore, these were still the days of the workhouse and any family in such dire circumstances as to find themselves in there would be immediately split up. Little wonder that neighbours helped each other, even though they were not that much better off than the families they were helping.

Ruby's father Ben was fortunate enough to have a job. He worked at Tinsley Park Colliery where he operated and maintained the cage. As a child she looked forward to going with her father on a

Friday to collect his pay. The route from their home to the colliery took them alongside the walls of Tinsley Park Cemetery. He would jokingly tell Ruby that he could hear voices coming from the cemetery complaining "Ooo. I'm on my own in here." In February 1943 Tinsley Park Colliery was closed by order of the Ministry of Fuel & Power, which controlled all coal mining operations in wartime. Ben was heartbroken!

Ruby was raised as an only child, which helped the family cope better in the harsh times than other families with several children. Even so, Ruby talks of how her mother looked forward to the day each quarter when Ben would receive his Army Reserve pay, as this would be a much needed boost to the family finances when things were getting tight.

Childhood entertainment in Ruby's young days was mostly self made. Any toys were either made by the father, or a small cheap toy was bought from a shop for some special occasion. Skipping, hop-scotch and hide-and-seek would be common games played, or something a bit more risqué, such as kick-can or knock-and-run, which was guaranteed to annoy the neighbours.And a neighbour was just as likely to tan a child's backside as their mother or father. A visit to the Darnall Cinema, or Little Dick as it was known to the children, for a Saturday matinee meant returning pop bottles to shops to get the halfpenny or penny deposit, until 3d (1p) or 4d (2p) had been collected, enough to get into the cinema.

Ruby notes, with some despair and annoyance, that these days children don't want traditional things such as bikes or compendiums of games. Instead they want, and expect, expensive items such TV games, laptops and mobile phones. Worse, when they're eighteen they want a car!

When she was fourteen her mother became pregnant again, though Ruby was not told, and she saw nothing to indicate her mother's pregnancy. There were no baby clothes lying around to suggest a new arrival. It is implausible these days to think that children, even younger than fourteen, know nothing of how babies come about. Sex education (or personal and social development) is now taught in junior schools, but in Ruby's youth the birds and the bees were not discussed in front of children. She was eventually told that a nurse would bring the baby in a bag.

On the night her mother went into labour she was sent to her friend Molly's house to sleep there, and Molly's mother attended Ruby's mother. The baby was delivered but only lived for four hours. There was no ante natal care then as there is today otherwise it would have been discovered that a cyst which had grown in the womb had burst and was killing the unborn baby. Even when the baby had died things were dealt with in silence in the matter of fact way of the time. An aunt wrapped the dead child in a blanket and took it to the cemetery to await interment at the next available burial, which meant the baby being buried in the grave of someone unconnected with the family, and it might be assumed that the family of the person they had just buried knew nothing of the additional corpse in the grave.

Such was Ruby's ignorance of puberty and human reproduction that even when her own menstrual cycle began, she didn't know what was happening to her. She only found out by talking to her mother one night when she was in bed, in the dark, and with her father at work on a night shift. Nor was Ruby the only girl unaware of the facts of life. A seventeen year old friend once confided to her that she had been told she was going to have a baby, but she had no idea where it was going to come from. And they say ignorance is bliss!

Things were far easier for Ruby to understand later. When she was seventeen her mother was pregnant again and this time Ruby knew all about the imminent arrival. But the outcome had a similar disastrous end. In her last week of pregnancy her mother decided to have the baby downstairs in their home in case of an air raid, the Second World War being now well underway. The house proud mother was moving furniture around when she felt a lurch inside her, and nothing after. The baby was stillborn. Ruby remained an only child.

But even knowing of her mother's pregnancy didn't mean she was fully aware of how it had come about, though she knew more than before. Ruby has said that she learnt about the facts of life through listening to her work colleagues at Flather's where she worked in World War Two. It must have been a shock to realise that babies weren't brought in bags by nurses.

Socially as a child, Ruby was involved with her mother in the Salvation Army movement, and she participated in many of the social and recreational activities on offer at the Queen Mary Road Salvation Army Hall at Manor Top. Every Monday evening, Ruby recalls, there was a lantern slide show, the cost of which was one penny. The slides would depict scenes from a well known story, and the operator would provide all the characters' voices.

Her father was not a committed Salvationist as her mother was, but he encouraged Ruby in her activities. Trips to the seaside were often arranged for the children, with Scarborough, Bridlington and Cleethorpes often the ports of call. On the way there and back the children would sing hymns to entertain themselves.

There were several sections of the movement that she and her young friends could participate in, but a drama group was one that she particularly enjoyed. She appeared in short religious plays at various venues in the city, and she particularly remembers performing with a friend at the Victoria Hall in Norfolk Street.

Such was her enthusiasm for the stage, and the quality of her performances, that she was encouraged to consider acting as a career.

FROM SHOP TO KITCHEN

An actor's life though was not to be for Ruby. Having left school, it was time to enter the world of work. Her first job was in A Jennings & Co's wallpaper shop in Fitzalan Square. This was followed by a job at Homealities groceries and pastry shop at 113 Ecclesall Road South, near All Saints' Church, a long way from the family home at the Manor. She worked there when the then Prime Minister, Neville Chamberlain, was attempting to secure peace with the German Chancellor Adolf Hitler. But with the threat of a war looming, Ruby remembers many wealthy Ecclesall residents panic buying and stocking up on food. This shop however closed down and Ruby then found herself working in Green's sweet shop on Division Street, which she managed in the owner's absence.

Her move to the sweet shop coincided with the onset of the Second World War. She was working there on the night of the first of the two major air raids over Sheffield, Thursday 12th December 1940. The shop normally closed at 8.00pm so as to catch people making their way to the Gaumont or the Cinema House in Barker's Pool. But during that afternoon word was going round that Sheffield would be hit that night. Mr Green had called into the shop to tell Ruby to lock the day's takings away and close at 7.00pm and go home. Ruby, having seen a mouse running round, decided to close at 6.00pm. During the raid the shop received a direct hit and was completely destroyed. Perhaps the mouse saved her life. To his relief though, when Mr Green visited his shop the day after, the takings were still safely locked away, in a toffee tin.

No such relief for eighteen years old Ruby who was now, like many other shop and office workers whose places of work had been obliterated, unemployed. She now had to sign on at the Labour Exchange on West Street (now the Jobcentre). When she arrived there were hundreds of equally unemployed blitz victims queuing all round the building.

Employment options were limited and restricted mostly to some kind of war work. Not fancying the women's Land Army or the armed forces, she was more or less instructed to go into munitions work at W T Flather's factory at Tinsley, and to report the following Monday for the 2.00 to 10.00pm shift.

Not knowing where the factory was, Ruby had to find the place. Due to the recent air raids of the Blitz there were no trams running. However several firms had laid on lorries to pick people up and take them to their places of work, in return for which the workers put a penny in a basin. She was quite taken aback by the number of different companies, one after the other, and feared she would never find Flather's. Eventually she did and having got off the lorry she had a good look round to get her bearings, and then waited for a lorry to take her back. Suddenly a Rolls Royce car pulled up and the driver asked her where she was going. She explained what she had been doing and why and the driver announced that he was Mr Flather's chauffer, and that he was on his way to pick up a concert party who were going to entertain workers at the factory. Lucky Ruby got a lift some of the way home in the firm's limousine, and saved the lorry fare!

Except for these first two extreme modes of transport, lorry and limousine, all other journeys to and from work were by tram. Despite the damage done to the tramway system in the Blitz, tramcars were soon running again, and were vital during the war for getting people about, especially to their work in the steel works and other factories. Fares were a penny or halfpenny, both less than 1p, and trams in those days carried mail boxes so that anyone could post a letter on them up to 10.00pm.

Come the Monday Ruby prepared to start work in a factory, not something she was greatly looking forward to. For some time she had been a secret smoker and had taken the odd fag from her father's cigarette packet. He had at times mentioned that he thought he had more cigarettes than he had, but must have known where they were going for before Ruby set off for work, he gave her five of his Woodbines.

What greeted her when she got to Flather's was not what she was prepared for and was quite alien to a naturally shy girl like Ruby. The place was smelly and noisy, and worse, she was made to wear a poorly fitting large overall and a mop cap. Being the new girl she was also laughed at in her work clothes. Ruby went home in tears. This was her baptism of fire! She didn't want to go back, but had no choice. Overnight her mother and a friend altered the overall to make it fit better and next day, instead of laughs, she got cat calls and wolf whistles, and instead of tears there were blushes. Ruby though was still naïve to such factory floor behaviour and language. Her first job at Flather's was in a rolling mill where munitions and components for war planes were manufactured. She recalls that she "quickly had to grow up in the works."

Before long Ruby would be married and expecting her first child. The baby, Graham, duly arrived and she had to leave to learn to be a mother. When Graham was old enough to be parted from his mum Ruby returned to Flather's, and her young son was looked after by her parents. She remained at Flather's for the duration of the war, though she was assigned to a different job, this time in the Test House, and on eleven hour day and thirteen hour night shifts. She had replaced a young man who had been called up for active service but, as she noted, she did not get the same wages the man had been paid. Equal pay for women was not a consideration in those days, even though it was more than obvious that women could do men's work. Even with the advances made in recent years to address this problem, there are still instances in 21st century Britain where women's pay does not match that of their male counterparts.

In this job Ruby worked on a lathe and would machine metal samples to be tested to destruction to ensure the material was fit for its intended purpose in the war effort. A popular wartime Gracie Fields song had a chorus *"She's the girl that makes the thing that drills the hole that holds the spring that drives the rod that turns the knob that works the thing-ummy-bob. She's the girl that makes the thing that holds the oil that oils the ring that takes the shank that moves the crank that works the thing-ummy-bob."* Ruby's work tested the thing-ummy-bob.

All wartime work was closely guarded, with some being very secret. Ruby's work in the Test House would be vital later in the war. She discovered that her work was connected with the famous Mulberry Harbour, essential to the success of the Normandy Landings in June 1944. It must have been work that she could get engrossed in as she once found she was working alone, everyone else having rushed to the air raid shelter during an attack. Despite the efforts of the German Luftwaffe, Ruby kept the flag flying!

Wartime life for most was not all about keeping the steelworks going night and day, but for Ruby, with her sheltered upbringing, it more of less was. Her husband away at war, a young son at home and long working hours, without household and domestic chores thrown in, didn't leave much time for any leisure. What few moments she did get were as often spent enjoying a film in Darnall's Lyric Picture House, possibly on a Saturday afternoon as was the practice at Flather's to close at noon. Many people did go to the cinema in those days, though there were other attractions. In October 1940 a German Messerschmitt 109 Fighter that had been shot down was on public display in Barker's Pool on the site of the former Albert Hall. All the proceeds from the 6d and 3d admission fees went to the Sheffield Newspapers War Fund.

As time passed at Flather's, Ruby was no longer the shy young thing she had been when she first started there, and could banter with the best of them. She well remembers Douglas Warrington, nicknamed Sandy because of his ginger hair, one of the men in the Test House, whom she and other women used to tease and embarrass. She finally left the company at the end of the war when her soldier husband, who she had not seen for four years, returned home.

Ruby and her husband then settled down to the usual kind of family life and more children were born. She was now in the role of a housewife, but when her children were old enough to come home from school by themselves, Ruby decided she would go back to work and, in 1953, got a part time job at Marks & Spencer working on the confectionery counter at their new store on The Moor (now Sainsbury's), but had to undergo her training at the store in Doncaster. The staff canteen and toilets in the store were on the second floor and, as her break was only fifteen minutes, it was almost time to return by the time she had got there. Ruby was very happy in this job but, now pregnant with her third child, the company's doctor decided that it was too much for her to climb the stairs and advised her to take time off to have her baby and return when she was able. This she did but decided not to return.

Having had her third child, Brendan, Ruby was a full time housewife again, and two more children, Kevin and Robert, were born. The children grew up and again Ruby decided she would go back to work. In 1970 she applied for a job as Kitchen Assistant at the English Steel Corporation's Management Training Centre at 32 Collegiate Crescent. She was the lucky last of twenty seven applicants and got the job. At this establishment graduates new to the company spent a year being tutored by company officials in the various aspects of the firm and the jobs they would be doing.

Here Ruby worked for Mrs Fisher, the Housekeeper, and the two got on very well with each other. The job involved preparing food and keeping the kitchen clean. On one occasion the Assistant

Cook went on leave and decided not to return. Mrs Fisher had a party of forty to cater for and asked Ruby if she would fill in and be trained to do the Assistant Cook's job. She was happy to oblige and the feeding of the forty went ahead without a hitch.

Mrs Fisher and her husband later went to work at the company's Training Centre at Brookfield Manor, Hathersage, and they asked Ruby if she would go with them, which she declined. She was then asked to fill the vacancy created by Mrs Fisher's departure, but this too she declined, and so a new Housekeeper was appointed to Collegiate Crescent.

Ruby's fourth son, Kevin, had a strong interest in cooking. He had been at the army's catering college and was at the time working as a Cook's Assistant at the Hen & Chickens public house in Castle Green, by the Court House on Castle Street. Having seen the advert for Assistant Cook at Brookfield Manor in The Star, he sent off an application, and got the job. Later however Mrs Fisher's husband died and, as she could not stay on alone, had to retire. Shortly after Kevin left as he found he could not work for their replacements.

Clifford House was once the home of Lieutenant Colonel Charles Clifford, Colonel of the 4th West Riding Royal Garrison Artillery Volunteers, whose headquarters were at the Norfolk Barracks on Edmund Road.

He was one of the owners of the Sheffield Daily Telegraph, forerunner of the Sheffield Weekly Telegraph, and co-founder of the Sheffield Evening Telegraph, forerunner of The Star.

He was a prominent citizen in Sheffield and, like many of his colleagues of similar status, was a benefactor of some public institutions. In his case he gave to the city the Charles Clifford Dental Hospital.

Ruby's new boss at Collegiate Crescent, Mrs Foster, would cook for the students and ask Ruby to cook for the directors. She was happy to do this but, as she discovered, and much to her annoyance, Mrs

Foster was taking the credit for Ruby's work. Naturally she was not happy about this and began to look for another job. Whilst serving her notice she worked at the company's Clifford House premises on Ecclesall Road South, due to the Collegiate Crescent site being redecorated. Here important clients, guests and dignitaries were entertained. On occasion civic furniture, bearing the city's Coat of Arms, was brought from Sheffield's Town Hall. At Clifford House Ruby worked for the Cook and Housekeeper Mrs Fay, who was more than a little partial to a drink!

Ruby was serving her notice when she got a cooking job at The Grove, a City Council Children's Home on Broomgrove Road, where Mr and Mrs Siddall were the Superintendents, the latter being a rather snobbish person, Ruby thought. The Siddalls' work with children had been rewarded by an invitation to a Buckingham Palace Royal Garden Party. On one occasion the Home received a visit from Sheffield's Lord Mayor Councillor Martha Stafford. The first person the Lord Mayor saw at the Home was Ruby whom she asked where the lavatory was as she was "peeing myself!" But apart from that display of down-to-earthness, Ruby says she was a most delightful person.

Ruby's last job was as Cook at Sheffield City Council's home for mentally and physically disabled children, Stafford House at Norfolk Park. There she stayed until her retirement at the age of sixty in 1982. Retirement though required as much hard work as working as she had an ill and elderly mother to look after. She did later take a small job cleaning the offices of her son Gregory's business. She was also on call for grandchildren duty, including taking them to and from the nearby Grace Owen Nursery School.

German bombs had first fallen on Sheffield in the Second World War on 18th August 1940. The first deaths occurred in a raid on the 29th. These and later air raids in August and September were isolated incidents, but doubtless made with the intention of locating potential targets and defences. The main air raids on the city, the Blitz, codenamed 'Operation Crucible', came in December, firstly on the night of Thursday 12th and into the early hours of the 13th, and secondly on the night of Sunday the 15th. Despite the German Luftwaffe having good intelligence about industrial targets in the east end, they chose on the first night to attack the city from the south west, concentrating on the city centre. Apart from the damage and destruction done to several buildings in The Moor, High Street and Angel Street areas by bombs, incendiaries and mines, there was also a lot of damage to houses along the route that the Luftwaffe's 300 or so bombers took, leaving the great steelworks of the east end, vital to Britain's war effort, relatively untouched. Air raid sirens sounded at 7.00pm on the 12th and the all clear didn't sound until 4.20am on the 13th, making this the longest single air raid endured by any British city outside London.

Why the Luftwaffe didn't hit the east end on this occasion is open to conjecture, and several theories have been suggested. But the east end didn't get away with it, for the German bombers returned on the night of Sunday 15th December, intent on putting the steelworks, engineering and munitions factories out of action. However the damage caused was insufficient to put a stop to war production and most works that were hit were able to continue working or were back in action within a day or two. The exception being Brown Bayleys where damage was such as to end production for about a week. As in the previous raid extensive damage was caused to housing in the areas surrounding the east end.

The Blitz claimed 602 lives and caused injuries to almost 1,600 people. Houses destroyed and damaged numbered around 80,000, leaving over 40,000 people homeless. Air raids continued throughout 1941, the last being on 28th July 1942. Air raids on Sheffield altogether killed 631 people and injured a total of 1,817.

FAMILY AND FRIENDS

Ruby's husband Frank was born on 5th April 1920, and lived with his parents, John and Cecilia Gascoigne, at 148 Coleford Road. The two met when she was seventeen. At the time Ruby was working in a corner shop on Coleford Road and Frank had come into the shop on an errand for his mother. He took an immediate liking to Ruby and after leaving the shop waited outside for her. He asked her out to the cinema and their relationship blossomed from there, though, as Ruby has said, they were just good friends at first. Romance and love came gradually over the rest of their time together.

Her father was very protective of her and watched her like a hawk. He did though get on well with Frank and he with him, and the two would often play cards and dominoes together. Frank had joined the Territorial Army, plumping for the Royal Engineers based at the Somme Barracks on Glossop Road. Everyone knew the Second World War was coming, and on Friday 1st September 1939 Frank and his Territorial colleagues were mobilised and told to report to Nether Edge School. They remained there until Sunday 3rd September, the day war was declared, before being transferred to Fulford Barracks at York. Ruby went with Frank's mother and father to see him at the Barracks and shortly after Frank was on his way to France as part of the British Expeditionary Force.

Within weeks the British army in France was being evacuated from Dunkirk, known as Operation Dynamo, and Frank was lucky enough to be on one of the last boats to leave. His parents had been very anxious about this and thought that he might have been killed. Frank's fifteen minutes of fame occurred when he arrived back at Dover. Frank was a strong swimmer and on the way back he had dived into the sea to save a soldier who had fallen in and couldn't swim. When he arrived at Dover he was completely naked. The arrival of the troops was filmed by a British Pathé newsreel team. When Frank arrived back in Sheffield on leave he and Ruby were informed that he had been seen in the film without any clothes. The two toured all the cinemas in Sheffield hoping to see the newsreel, and it wasn't until the evening before Frank had to rejoin his unit that they saw the film in Darnall Cinema. The same footage was seen many years later on television in a programme of wartime Prime Minister Winston Churchill's memoirs. This time it was seen by millions and over the next few days several of Frank and Ruby's friends were telephoning them to say that they had seen Frank naked on the telly.

Later that year Frank's unit was stationed in Liverpool. He was there on the night of Sunday 15th December 1940 when Sheffield was subjected to the second of its two blitz air raids. His home on Coleford Road received a direct hit and both his parents were killed. The same bomb killed several Air Raid Wardens who were in their station which was attached to the end-of-terrace house. Another Warden, who should have been in the station, had been sent with a message to another station, and therefore escaped the fate of his colleagues. He was one of Ruby's uncles.

The Imperial War Graves Commission's "Roll of Honour of Civilian War Dead in the United Kingdom 1939-45" for the County Borough of Sheffield shows that Frank's parents John Thomas, 50, and Cecilia, 46, were both Air Raid Wardens and were killed at the Warden's station. Also killed in the ARW station were Wardens John Thomas Appleby, 60, of 74 Phillimore Road, Joseph Armstrong, 44, of 56 Phillimore Road, his wife Leonora, 41, Frederick Brown, 38, of 71 Coleford Road, Lawrence Hall, 38, of 146 Coleford and Victor George Thomas Salisbury, 42, of 300 Greenland Road.

On this night Ruby recalls how she was at home with her mother, their father not having returned home from work. They said their prayers and hoped the raid would be less damaging than the one two days earlier. When her father eventually returned home at

4.00am, he was deeply upset at the devastation he had witnessed and all the innocent people killed. A hardened old soldier, he nevertheless cried.

The following day Ruby and her parents made their way down Prince of Wales Road to see if their relations were all right. This road had suffered during the raid and was strewn with debris and burning tram cars split in two. It was when they got to Coleford Road that they heard the news of Frank's parents. People enduring an air raid had few options for protecting themselves. There were several communal air raid shelters about that people could go to. Some, defying Hitler to the last, preferred to stay in their home and took shelter under stairs and in cellars. Others had an Anderson shelter in their garden that was, in part, below ground level. Ruby's family had one of these and it was a daily ritual for her father to drain the shelter of the water that had collected, and for blankets and bedding to be aired, ready for the next night's occupation.

"It seemed as though they had followed the tram lines up from Darnall because Prince of Wales Road looked absolutely devastated...The tram lines...were all blown up and the cars were all smashed up. Trams just shattered. The rails all twisted and bent up... trams all over the place."

It was the practice in the army that if a town was being attacked, soldiers from that town would be given a forty-eight hour pass to go and see their family. Frank had been given such a pass and was at a railway station when he was given a telegram from his Commanding Officer informing him of his parents' death. His thoughts can only be imagined. He came home to a scene that showed only piles of bricks where his home had been. His parents were buried in Darnall Cemetery on Christmas Eve.

His eleven year old brother Herbert, and fifteen year old sister Cecilia, who had been sent to an air raid shelter across the road during the raid, were now orphaned. They were staying with their mother's parents. Frank's father had been a member of the local lodge of the Royal Antediluvian Order of Buffaloes and they arranged for Herbert to be cared for at the Order's orphanage in Harrogate. Cecilia though lied about her age and joined the Auxiliary Territorial Service, being stationed in Hull

The fortunes of the two siblings proved to be quite different. Cecilia later fell pregnant to a soldier and the two were married. The soldier was the son of an ex Lord Mayor of Hull, and head of one of Hull's biggest fishing businesses. She died in childbirth aged thirty seven. Many years later Cecilia's son contacted Ruby quite out of the blue. Neither knew the other existed and it was only due to the son's interest in finding out about his mother's relatives that he found his uncle Frank and his family.

Herbert though had been well cared for by the Buffaloes and had acquired a reasonable bank account, courtesy of the members of the Order. On leaving the orphanage he was taken in by his mother's parents who, it transpired, only wanted him for his money. The good clothes he had been wearing were now reduced to not much more than rags. He was most unhappy and, aged seventeen, he asked Ruby if he could live with her and she was kind enough to take him in. He later joined the army and went his own way, raising his own family. He died in Sheffield in 2010.

It was just before Christmas 1940 that Frank asked Ruby to marry him, and she said "Yes". The marriage was scheduled to take place at St Swithun's Church, Manor, on Easter Saturday, 12th April 1941. With Frank stationed in Liverpool, Banns were read at St Swithun's Church and at Liverpool Cathedral. Three days before the wedding Frank's unit was despatched to Armagh, Northern Ireland. He had to quickly appeal to his Commanding Officer for leave to be married, which was immediately granted. He travelled back on Thursday night, arriving in Sheffield the following day. He had also been given a suit in which to be married. This though was poorly fitting, but was quickly altered by Ruby's mother and her friend. Her father also lent Frank his new shoes.

The couple were duly married, with Ruby given away by a tearful father. The reception was held at the Salvation Army Hall on Queen Mary Road, with ladies of the Sally Army waiting on serving a meal of offal, tongue, pickles and salad. The wedding cake was decorated with rice paper, as were many in ration book Britain. This was followed by an evening for family and friends at Ruby's home, necessary in case the air raid sirens sounded. Frank had been granted a week's leave, during which he had to sort out his father's affairs, ensure that his young brother and sister were properly catered for, and to sort out insurances for his new bride. He then said goodbye to his wife and returned to Northern Ireland.

Frank had a short spell of leave between Christmas 1941 and the New Year, which was the first time the two had seen each other since their wedding. They made the most of it and Frank again returned to Northern Ireland. He had forty eight hours' leave a short while later, from which his unit was posted overseas to a warmer climate, tropical wear was in his kit bag. These few days they had together would be the last they saw of each other until the end of the war. On 7th October 1942 their first child Graham was born at home, an event which made Ruby believe that she and Frank had a good New Year's Eve.

The next months Ruby spent at home caring for her baby boy but before long she returned to work at Flather's. At the end of the war Frank returned and Ruby left her job to take up the duties and chores of a housewife. She and Frank had not seen each other for the better part of four years, and had a lot of catching up to do. Though the war was over Frank, like his brother soldiers, was on the Army Reserve List.

The situation in Germany and Eastern Europe was politically delicate and trouble could flare up at any time.

Apart from the hardships living in wartime brought, there was the constant terror of air raid devastation, whether at work or at home. The sirens could go at any time, and often did, even though Sheffield was not the target. In many works no one went into the air raid shelters until the bombs started dropping, production was that important. At Flather's though workers had to go to the shelter when the sirens sounded. The shelter had been specially made and was approached down a set of stairs that led into a long tunnel. Easy to get into in the daytime, but hazardous at night in the blackout

The tunnel had benches with a curtain at the end, behind which was a bucket, which served as the toilet. People had to sing or whistle when using it in order to disguise the splashing of the wee entering the bucket. If the sirens sounded at mealtime the food would be taken with them. Many hours could be spent in the tunnel until the all clear sounded, so people had to make their own entertainment, or sleep if they could.

The air raid sirens sounded whether the raid was on Sheffield or not. German bombers had to fly over Sheffield to get to the Lancashire cities of Manchester and Liverpool to do their damage there. Naturally Sheffielders would be glad that their names weren't on the bombs, but sad that someone else's were. The planes flying over Sheffield to another city were heavily laden with bombs and had a far deeper sound than when they were flying back much lighter. But this did not mean they posed any less threat. Often they would still be carrying bombs which they would drop over Sheffield just to get rid of them. A moonlit night was as bad as daylight as the River Don, the canal and the train lines would reflect the moonlight, indicating just where the industrial targets were. People would hope that this night wasn't their night.

Young people these days think nothing of joining a queue or camping out to ensure they get a ticket for a pop concert or catch a glimpse of a film star at a premiere. But queue for food? This is what happened in wartime Britain and the end of a nightshift might signal the start of a queuing shift. Many items such as food and clothing were rationed and with only a specific amount of foods per person allowed each week, it was always available. But things not on ration would cause queues to form outside shops in the hope of being able to obtain whatever it was the shop had. Word would soon go round that so-and-so's had something and a queue would start very early. Ruby's mum once went to the local fishmonger at 4.00am to queue for half a rabbit. The shop didn't open until 9.00am but she got her quarry. It wasn't for her though. She swapped it with a neighbour for a tablet of soap! Such was the way of life then. It was not uncommon for Ruby to finish a 13 hour night shift at 6.00am, get on a tram and go to a shop and queue until 9.00am for five cigarettes. Flather's had a policy of always having cigarettes in stock in their canteen, rationed of course to 20 per employee. With Ruby being on nights, the nurse would ensure that Ruby got her quota, but she always fetched her Capstan Full Strength.

These too were the days of the spiv, some local bloke who was always able to get something that people wanted – for a price. One such man worked at Flather's and Ruby had several black market things off him. He managed to get her a very good coat, and he was a good provider of sides of bacon. Another was the father of one of Ruby's friends, a policeman.

Though Ruby knew Frank was coming home, but not exactly when, it was a bit of a shock when he came through the back door at three in the morning, the two not having seen each other for over four years. Having been stationed in the Middle East and in India, Franks' skin had darkened. His return was the first opportunity he'd had to see his son Graham. It was also the first time three year old Graham had seen his father in the flesh and his appearance seemed strange to the young boy because Frank no longer looked as he did in the photograph Ruby had of him. To celebrate the home coming, Ruby's mother had bought a chicken for a welcoming meal.

Their re-union, though much welcomed, wasn't easy straight away. Ruby was not the same person she had been. She was now wiser to the world, and had lived outside the realms of her sheltered upbringing. Like Frank, she had experienced many life changing events that the war had unleashed. She had also made many new male acquaintances during the war at Flather's, which made Frank a little jealous when they spoke to her in the street. This was not uncommon amongst married couples meeting up again after so long, and many marriages ended in divorce because neither husband nor wife, nor life, was the same as it had been before the war. But Ruby and Frank sorted themselves out and went on to have a happy life together and raise their family. On 6th October 1946 their second son Gregory was born. The timing of this birth makes Ruby reckon that she and Frank had another good New Year's Eve.

On his return Frank had two weeks' pay. Luckily he found a job straight away with a demolition firm knocking down what remained of the buildings that Hitler's bombs had failed to completely flatten. He then went to work driving coal lorries for King Cole & Co at their coal depot on Darnall Road. He was there for about two years before going to work for the Tempered Rubber Company, a subsidiary of the Tempered Springs Company. This was a job that Frank liked very much, but the company was later sold to Dunlop.

Dunlop, however, were to close the factory and move production to Skelmersdale in Lancashire. Frank was offered a job there, but this would have meant the family moving to a new housing estate Dunlop had built at Southport. It transpired though the offer was not as good as it first seemed and so Frank turned it down, resulting in his redundancy. Frank wept when he saw the cheque for his redundancy pay, he never having had so much money. The home benefited by having some new furniture. Not one to remain unemployed, Frank got a job at the Blackburn Meadows Power Station, site of 'Salt and Pepper', the famous, but now demolished, Tinsley Cooling Towers. He was to remain there until the station closed in the 1970s.

Blackburn Meadows Power Station was the third electricity generating station built by Sheffield Corporation. It was opened in October 1921 by HRH Prince Albert, Duke of York (who would become King George VI). The station was later much enlarged with the new extension being opened by the Prince Albert's younger brother HRH Prince George, Duke of Kent, on 6th April 1933.

The power station became part of the nationalised Central Electricity Generating Board in 1948 and closed in the early 1970s. It was demolished a decade later, though it was considered too dangerous to demolish the two cooling towers at the side of the recently built Tinsley Viaduct. These were finally demolished by controlled explosion in the early hours of 24th August 2008.

As a working teenager Frank had always given his wages to his mother, but he kept overtime payments and bonuses for himself. With these he bought his mother a new washing machine for the then staggering sum of twenty-nine guineas (£30.45). Miraculously this survived the bomb damage on his parents' home, with only the wringer rollers not working. It found its way however into the home of his mother's parents and when he asked for it back they refused to part with it. It was only after the war, when Ruby was expecting her second child, that the washing machine was returned. A friend of Frank's was able to repair the rollers, and the washing machine served the family for several years.

Frank and Ruby lived with Ruby's mother, she being now widowed. In 1947 her mother rented a larger house on Main Road at Darnall and the three of them moved there with the children. Her mother ran the house as a boarding house for single men, and she did the cooking and the shopping whilst Ruby did the cleaning in return for living there rent free.

In time Ruby's mother married a Manor newsagent and went to live with him at his house on Fretson Road, leaving the Main Road house to Frank and Ruby. The new husband had died of cancer within two years and Ruby's mother decided to move to a smaller house on the same road. Frank and Ruby and the boys moved into the house that Ruby's mother had vacated, and it was here that the other boys were born, Brendan on 3rd February 1953, Kevin on 13th January 1957 and Robert on 21st September 1961. Ruby was now a full time mother.

Prior to the establishment of the National Health Service in 1948, all professional health care had to be paid for, including the services of a family doctor. Graham's and Gregory's births would have necessitated the doctor charging for his visits to Ruby – all her children were born at home. Her doctor had known Ruby since her childhood and because of this he waived his charges for the delivery of Graham and Gregory, telling Ruby to give his fee to the babies. Brendan, Kevin and Robert, being born after 1948, came without charge.

Ruby's mother was not done with marrying. Her third husband died of a heart attack, this marriage also lasting about two years. These last two marriages had been church weddings with Frank giving the bride away. He would joke that he kept giving her away, but she kept coming back!

One boarder at the house was a Polish man named Viktor Gruza. He had been exiled from his own country during the Second World War and served with the Royal Air Force, as did many of his countrymen. He had decided to stay in Sheffield after the war and worked as an engineer, which had been his job in Poland. His command of the English language was limited, and included a few rude words and Anglo-Saxon expletives, but Ruby taught him English which helped him tremendously in his work and social life.

He had met a woman named Irene Springthorpe who lived in Derby. Her family were related to the Wilkinson Sword family. The two eventually married and moved to Buffalo in New York State in the United States of America. Here Viktor worked for the Ford Motor Company, becoming a manager and was able to amass some reasonable wealth. Whenever they came back to England to visit Irene's mother, they always came to Sheffield to see Frank and Ruby. When Viktor retired he and Irene moved to Saratosa in Florida and they continued corresponding with Frank and Ruby. In time they discovered through Irene's mother that Irene had died, and they later lost contact with Viktor.

Frank loved his job at the power station and was quite sad when it closed and a lot of his workmates lost their jobs. His time working on power stations though was not at an end. He spent the next two years with colleagues visiting a number of stations in the area doing maintenance work. After a couple of years, aged sixty-two, he took early retirement to help Ruby look after her aged mother, Lavinia, who was now suffering from Alzheimer's Disease and in need of constant attention.

The boys were by now married and raising their own families. Graham married Gillian, the two being old school friends, and had Daryll, Janine and Kieron. Gregory, who built up his own successful business, married Andrea and had Dene, Lee, Mark and Jane. Brendan married Carole and had Sarah and Andrew. Kevin, a chef and now a director of Country Fresh Foods of Sheffield, married Lynn and had Nicola and Liam.

Robert, a care worker and trade union official with Unison, married Dawn, a nursing sister, and had Carly and Neil. Kevin's marriage ended in divorce and he later married Lisa and they now have two sons, Jonathan and Ben

Blackburn Meadows Power Station's closure in the early 1970s was at the beginning of a period that saw much of the industry in and around Sheffield gradually disappear, though for different reasons. Blackburn Meadows, like its fellow station at Neepsend, were built at a time when the city of Sheffield was expanding rapidly, with ever increasing demands on the new medium of electricity. Since the 1960s however, new and much larger power stations had now been built to serve national rather than local needs. These were located close to the coal fields of South and West Yorkshire and Nottinghamshire, and on the banks of rivers such as the Trent and the Ouse, both bigger than the Don. Constrained by the Blackburn Meadows Sewage Treatment Works and the railway to the north, the River Don and the canal to the south, the M1 motorway to the west and factories to the east, there was no room for expansion at Blackburn Meadows. It could not be modernised and enlarged, and closure was the only viable option. Forty years on and the site is now destined for development as a power station using bio-mass fuels, safer for the environment.

By contrast the closure of the coal mines and the steelworks in the 1980s were the result of the purely political and ideological policies of the Conservative government. The closures were wholesale and sudden, with no thought for the impact these would have on families and communities, large or small. Both industries were the subject of national strikes, with the coal strike of 1984 being a most divisive one. It caused great unhappiness one way or another. Frank and Ruby had friends where there were miners and policemen in the same family. Their respective duties pitted them against each other, and in some cases relatives suddenly became enemies. Graham at the time lived in the strong mining community of Kiveton Park near Sheffield, and it was not uncommon for police to chase striking miners through his garden. The strike caused much stress and sadly several families broke up, and over twenty five years on the bitterness is still there.

Ruby's extended family now boasts fifteen grandchildren, twenty great grandchildren and one great great grandchild.

There were more great grandchildren in December 2011 when Kevin gained two more grandchildren. Ruby and Lisa's mother Eileen, or Eiloo as she is known to everyone, have become good friends and often enjoy outings and short breaks together. One of Ruby's great joys is going to stay with Eiloo at the caravan she shares with Kevin and Lisa.

Ruby and her two school friends, Molly and Margaret, remained close and kept in touch with each other almost up to the present. Molly and Ruby were as sisters, with their families being neighbours. Their mothers would come to the aid of each other when one or the other was ill or in need of some help. Molly's family were Roman Catholic but this did not matter to the young girls. Molly would accompany Ruby to the Salvation Army and Ruby do likewise when Molly went to confession at St Theresa's Roman Catholic Church on Prince of Wales Road. Molly married and later moved to Lincoln. Her husband had been at Arnhem in Holland in the Second World War, part of Operation Market Garden, the Allies' ill fated campaign to capture the bridge across the River Rhine there. He returned to Arnhem every year to take part in the service of remembrance. On his last visit he died. Molly unfortunately went blind though was still able to keep in contact with Ruby until her death in 2011.

The other childhood friend, Margaret, was at the Pupil Teacher Centre, and Margaret later became a teacher. She always took an interest in Ruby's children, and later grandchildren, but never married and had a family herself. In recent times Ruby grew concerned about Margaret as contact seemed to dwindle and, at the time of writing, has ceased, leaving Ruby to believe that Margaret has resigned herself to old age. But Ruby still sends cards wishing her lifelong friend well.

On a holiday to the Isle of Man shortly after the war Frank and Ruby met a young couple who were to become good friends, though not before a strange introduction. In the boarding house were a young man and woman who did not speak or mix with any of the other guests. One day a party of the guests went on a day trip to Dublin, but the couple did not go.

The Republic of Ireland at the time was not subject to the same rationing that was prevalent in the United Kingdom and the day trippers were able to spend almost all their holiday money buying such luxuries as silk stockings, chocolate, tinned fruit and salmon. Things that had not been seen in England for many years.

Eventually the young man spoke to Frank and Ruby in his Irish accent. He wanted to know why they had bought goods in Dublin, denying them to Irish people. They explained the situation, and that such items were scarce in England. It transpired that the couple's reaction to the English guests was due to them having been brought up to hate English people, being told that the English were cannibals and had no culture. Their parents had been around during the days of the Irish uprising, little more than a generation earlier, and had grown to dislike the English. With the ice being broken Frank, Ruby and Ada and Brendan, the Irish couple, got on well during the rest of the holiday and were able to educate each other as to their respective lives and their countries.

1953 was the year of Queen Elizabeth II's coronation and Ada and Brendan came to England, having been invited by Frank and Ruby, who was now pregnant with her third son, to watch the coronation on television. The television, a rare sight in homes in those days, had been bought specially for the occasion. By comparison with today's fifty-inch, plasma screen, 3D, HD, multi screen, satellite, remote control televisions, Frank and Ruby's was a twelve-inch chunky piece of furniture with a large magnifier in front of the screen. High tech indeed for the time! Ada and

Brendan, who stayed with Frank and Ruby for two days, went on to visit several places in England, and were given a coronation mug to take back to Ireland with them. The television was one of the first in the street, as her father's radio had been many years earlier. It was a novelty to more than just the Gascoigne family. Often friends and neighbours would arrive to watch a programme, bringing with them their own chairs and sandwiches. But they didn't stay to clean up after them. That was left to Frank and Ruby.

Ada and Brendan later invited Frank and Ruby to their wedding in Dublin. Not surprisingly Frank and Ruby were the only non Catholics present. Ruby was surprisingly asked to give a speech at the reception. Though taken aback, she rose to the occasion and spoke of the barriers that had been broken down, and the friendship that had built up. The only down side to the occasion appears to have been when the coronation mug was brought out, which upset one of the happy couples' parents.

The newlyweds honeymooned in London and took the opportunity to come to Sheffield to visit Frank and Ruby, she having recently given birth to the third son Brendan. Another lifelong friendship had come about and the two families have had many holidays in each others' countries. The friendship continues, though Brendan died in 2010. This friendship was further strengthened when Frank and Ruby took Brendan's pram to Dublin on one of their holidays. They gave the pram to Ada and Brendan and their three children each made use of it in turn. The pram was later donated to a home for unmarried mothers.

In October 2011 Ruby made a nostalgic visit to Dublin to see her old friend Ada, and her family, accompanied by Kevin and Lisa. This was Kevin's first visit to Ireland since his childhood, and he well remembers Brendan teaching him to count to ten in Irish, something he can still do!

Ruby's mother Lavinia and
her sister Aunty Beatty in their
unflattering First World War
Land Army girls' uniform

Stand House Council School, opened on 1st October 1931, by George
Lathan,Labour MP for Sheffield Park 1929 to 1931 & 1935 to 1942.
The first head teacher was Miss Dorothy T Hartley

The former Pupil Teacher
Centre, Holly Street. The
rear of Sheffield City Hall
is off to the right

Ruby with her father on holiday at Blackpool…

Ruby's father Ben in his Home Guard uniform

Ruby's parents on holiday in Cleethorpes in 1939. The Second World War wasn't too far away

Ruby with some of her W T Flather wartime colleagues. Back: Rhoda, Margaret, Jim, Douglas 'Sandy' Warrington. Middle: Mary, Daisy, Ruby. Front: Gordon, the apprentice.

Like any other Sheffield steel works, W T Flather's was on the Luftwaffe's hit list. This damage was caused during a 1940 air raid, but failed to put the firm out of action for any length of time

A bomb damaged Coleford Road following the raid of Sunday 15th December 1940

Frank aged 20 at his Coleford Road home. In the background is the tower of St Alban's church which was also destroyed in the air raid that destroyed his home

Ruby's wartime National Identity Card. UK citizens had to have their ID Card with them at all times during, and even after, the war

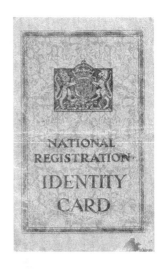

Oxydol, a popular soap powder of the 1940s, was the housewives' choice

Frank and Ruby's wedding. At the side of Ruby is Frank's sister Cecilia.
Other guests include Frank's uncles and cousins

Frank, right, and comrades stationed in Jerusalem, 1942

A Bush Model 22 television set, the kind that the 1953 coronation would have been watched on. The 9" screen necessitated a large magnifier being placed in front of the screen so that everyone gathered round could watch the programme

New friends Ada and Brendan on the Isle of Man.

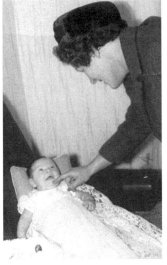

Ruby with her first grandchild Daryll

Ruby aged seventeen outside Frank's Coleford Road home

Despite her broken leg, Ruby still enjoyed a good chinwag

Graham's and Gill's wedding with Frank and Ruby left. Ruby's smile hides the pins holding her dress together

A slim line Robert as a mummy and Ruby as an angel at one of the Gascoignes' famous fancy dress parties

Gregory Gascoigne

Il Vino flows freely at Ruby's first taste of Spain

Frank and Ruby enjoy a day trip to Cleethorpes, August 1939

Frank, Ruby, Graham and Gregory enjoy a holiday at Rhyl

Ruby's mother Vinnie receives her prize for winning the Grandest Grandmother Competition from a Redcoat who would become TV's Freddie 'Parrot Face' Davies

A 1938 advert for a Model F Servis washing machine. The latest in laundry technology

An Easter Parade about to get underway at High Hazels Park, Darnall, in the 1950s

WHAT WITH ONE THING AND ANOTHER

A full life has many events in it. Some, though annoying and frustrating, and even serious at the time, are looked back on with amusement and provide a source of laughter in later years. Ruby's life has witnessed several such events, as she recalls.

At the age of seventeen Ruby had booked a seat to see a film at The Lyric Picture House on Main Road at Darnall. Having booked for the second house, as the second screening was then known, she was waiting by a wall across the road from the cinema. Some children were playing on the wall when suddenly the wall collapsed onto Ruby's foot, crushing her toes. She was taken into the cinema's foyer and attended to whilst an ambulance was called. Shortly after, the first house film goers came out, amongst whom were her mother and father, though they did not notice that the injured person was their daughter. It was only later, when the police arrived at her home to inform her parents of the accident, that they learned of Ruby's misfortune. Such was the injury that she lost the ends of some toes and became gangrenous, and had to learn to walk again. When Frank returned from Dunkirk he acquired a wheelchair so that he could take her out and about. Ruby had to be collected by ambulance every day and taken to the hospital. So many times did she make this journey that she reckons she knew all the ambulance drivers by name.

Not long before the end of the Second World War Ruby and her young son Graham had moved to Stonecliffe Close, a cul-de-sac near The Circle off Prince of Wales Road. She had written to Frank to let him know of the move. His eventual return to his family came in the middle of the night, but he had no idea where Stonecliffe Close was. He had to knock up several houses to find out, and finally got home at three o'clock in the morning.

The house at Main Road, Ruby's mother's new house, run as

a boarding house, which they had all moved to in 1947, had a very large cellar which, being cool, was excellent for storing food. However it was also prone to flooding. Frank though had a stirrup pump and decided he would pump out the water. He led a pipe upstairs to the kitchen sink and left Graham in charge of it. He however took his eye off the sink and the pipe came out, flooding the kitchen and making its way back into the cellar.

One of the boarder's at this house, a man named George, decided that he would enter the haulage business and bought himself a five ton drop side lorry with which to transport materials for building contractors. He offered the family a trip to Blackpool in it, though the lorry had not been built for comfort and convenience. George, Frank and Gregory were in the cab with Ruby, Graham and her mother on the back. Ruby was of the opinion that the people they passed must have thought they were gypsies. When they arrived in Blackpool those on the back were filthy and the party daren't go where the crowds were but had to find some secluded spot where they could wash themselves in the sea. The journey home was no less pleasant, but at least it was in the dark so no one could see them.

The winter of 1947 is noted as being one of the worst on record for low temperature, fall of snow and the length of time it lay on the ground. At the time Frank and Ruby were living on Stonecliffe Close. People were quite literally snowed in and traffic could not get much beyond the main roads. Worse, Frank and Ruby and their neighbours were running very short of coal. Frank, then working at King Cole, went and asked his boss if he could borrow a ten ton lorry and load it with coal to take his neighbours. With permission granted he took the lorry as far as he could get and then carried hundredweight sacks of coal from Prince of Wales Road to the houses on Stonecliffe Close, much to the relief of everyone. They say one good deed deserves another. Frank's good deed was repaid when he went to pay his boss for the coal. The boss simply said "Have it on me".

During the war, due to fuel rationing, car owners had been advised to lay their cars up for the duration and, to make things difficult for the enemy should they have invaded, remove the wheels and support the car on bricks. After the war a woman friend of Frank and Ruby's had the chance to buy such a car and Frank went with her to check it over. A woman owning a car in those days would have been quite a novelty. Everything seemed all right and Frank decided that a day trip to Blackpool would put the car through its paces so off they went, Frank, Ruby, the two boys and the car's new owner.

All was going well until they got to the Woodhead Road. Frank noticed a wheel running in front of them. It suddenly dawned on him that it was a wheel from their car. It turned out that a wrong wheel had been fitted on a wrong hub. The party never made it to Blackpool.

Frank bought his own car, a Ford, after the war from a butcher. A day trip to Morecambe was arranged for Frank and Ruby, her mother, Graham and Gregory. All was gong well until the journey along the East Lancs road when the car had a flat tyre. The road however had recently been resurfaced and the temperature on the day was so hot that the tarmac was melting and sliding towards the sides of the road. It was not easy for Frank to get the jack under the car as it kept sinking into the tarmac.

Being in smart clean clothes, Frank had to get a blanket from the car to kneel on. But this got tar stuck to it and had to be discarded, being thrown over a hedge. Try as he might, he could not change the wheel, and so had to walk into Morecambe to get assistance, though Morecambe was much further away than a passing motor cyclist had told him. Eventually he returned with help and the wheel was changed, though Frank was the only one of the party who managed to get to Morecambe that day.

This was though not the end of the family's motoring woes Ruby remembers. On one occasion Lavinia, Ruby's mother, went to stay at Butlins with a friend. Frank and Ruby took her in their car, but on the way back the car broke down. Unable to fix the problem, Frank phoned the AA who, after some time, advised him that there was a garage about two miles away, but they would have to try and push the car there. They arrived exhausted, only to find that the garage owner could not fix the car because a component needed to be ordered. Worse, there were no taxis in the area and no railway station.

In the end the garage owner said he would lend them one of his cars which they could return the following week when they collected their own car. The car on offer had certainly seen better days. It was covered inside and out in cobwebs, and had been a home for several chickens and other creatures. It was also very slow, the journey home taking about five hours. The garage owner was very anxious that they should not forget to return the car, but Brendan, who was with them, reminded the owner that he now had a better car in his possession.

The family moved to Harborough Drive when Graham and Gregory were children. This was a newly built house on the Manor Park estate and all the houses looked alike. When the two boys were out playing, Ruby would put a vase in the front window so that the boys would know which house was theirs. One day new curtains had been fitted to the windows and the vase was removed. Ruby decided to see if the boys would notice and would by now know which house was theirs and was peeping through the curtains. She saw the two looking at the houses in turn to determine where they lived. In time there was a timid knock at the door. When she opened it there stood Graham and Gregory. Graham, then an attendee at the Salvation Army Sunday School, opened his mouth and shouted "What've you shifted the bloody statue for?"

In due course Frank had a garage built by the side of the house. This was followed by the provision of a drive. Whilst this was being laid Graham and Gregory were kicking a ball when it went onto the garage roof. Gregory climbed up to get it, but in coming down he fell and landed in a tub of tar, covering him from head to foot. Ruby had to scrub him and use all sorts of cleaning agents to get him clean again.

When Brendan was eleven years old it was discovered that he had been playing truant from Stand House School for some time. As far as Ruby was concerned everything was normal. He left for school in the morning, came home for dinner and went back, and came home in the afternoon. On one occasion he came home at lunchtime soaking wet and told Ruby when she asked that he had been to the school's outside toilet and was caught in a thunderstorm. Ruby kept him off school for the rest of the day but next morning decided to take him to school so she could apologise for Brendan's absence the previous afternoon. To Ruby's astonishment the teacher informed her that Brendan had not been seen for the last eight or nine weeks.

Ruby, at the time pregnant with Robert, tried and tried to find out why her son was not attending school, and the worry was not making her pregnancy any easier. In the course of time it transpired that a school bobby (or attendance inspector), who was also a near neighbour, had seen Brendan on several occasions and had been told that he had had chicken pox and measles, quite believable as these were common amongst school children. It also came to light that Brendan had spent days in City Road Cemetery talking to the grave diggers. The real reason for his absence though was not forthcoming and he would simply tell Ruby to forget it. His teacher confided to Ruby that Brendan was quite advanced at school, and ahead of other children in the class. She was not too worried about him having to catch up. She tried to put Ruby at ease by telling her she would get to the bottom of the matter.

By now it was the six weeks summer holiday, shortly after which Ruby gave birth to Robert. Brendan went back to school and in time there was a parents' evening where Ruby discovered the reason for Brendan's truancy. He simply didn't want his mother to have any more children. It was obviously such a big thing to him that caused him great anxiety, but which disappeared once the new baby arrived.

When Graham left school he entered an apprenticeship which required him to attend college each week. To ease his travel Frank and Ruby bought him a moped. Alas one day he had an accident on Prince of Wales Road, fortunately not serious enough to warrant him going to hospital. Ruby though decided that a visit to the doctor was in order. When he removed his shirt it was discovered that he was covered with chicken pox, which his brothers Brendan, Kevin and Robert were all suffering with at home, genuinely in Brendan's case.

Graham decided to get rid of the moped and bought instead a motor bike and sidecar. He and his girlfriend Gillian were fond of one particular Sheffield pop group at the time, The Whirlwinds, and used to go to various pubs and clubs to see them play at least once a week. On one occasion the group were playing at a venue in Barnsley and the two set off with Gillian, in her short skirt with several under layers, popular at the time, in the sidecar. Off went the bike with Graham on it, leaving Gillian behind in the sidecar. Frank came to the rescue and secured the sidecar back to the motor bike. They enjoyed their night out but, returning home along Broughton Lane, the motor bike and sidecar parted company again.

A keen footballer and member of the Woodbourn Road Youth

Team, Graham once broke his leg and had to spend several weeks in traction. He was off work for about six months, during which period he had no wages. His team mates organised a charity night at Midhill Working Men's Club on East Bank Road to raise money to help him, and secured the services of comedian Paul Shane. This was in the days when Shane was a working men's club entertainer, before he achieved fame in BBC TV's "Hi-De-Hi". A good night was had by all, and a good sum of money was had by Graham.

Gardens are makeshift football pitches for most young soccer mad boys, and the Gascoignes' was no different. Theirs had a bush in corner, which Kevin fell into one day, cutting his face quite badly. The only way doctors at the hospital could dress the wounds was to fully bandage his face. With holes left in the dressing only for his eyes and mouth he looked like the invisible man. During the night the bandage slipped so as to cover his eyes and mouth, but he steadfastly refused to let anyone re-arrange the dressing. He remained in this guise until the bandages were removed at the hospital.

Robert was only three months old when he got his first taste of hospitals. He had been taken ill with catarrh in his windpipe, causing severe breathing difficulties, and had to be rushed into the Children's Hospital Thornbury Annexe at Ranmoor. With various tubes attached to him doctors were able to remove the blockage. But he was lucky. Another hour, Frank and Ruby were informed, and he could have died. The problem stayed with him for several years and at times he would be out playing when he would start gasping for air and have to be given drugs to make his breathing easier.

But this was not the only worry for Ruby as far as Robert was concerned. As a child of about seven years he attended a bonfire and came away with a swollen leg. He had apparently been bitten by a grass snake, no doubt fleeing the bonfire. This though was no minor injury and he was ill for some time. A few years later he was with friends at Beauchief on the Sheffield Round Walk when the path they were following split. Not being sure which path to follow they approached a house to ask directions but were met with a terrifying surprise. The owner of the house had decided that actions speak louder than words and shot the boys with a 12 bore shotgun. All of them received several pellet wounds.

Nor was that the end of it. Robert had a passion for food and would not stop eating, causing him to become overweight. Frank and Ruby tried a number of methods to get him to eat less, even to the extent of putting combination locks on the fridge. But a determined Robert soon discovered the way in and carried on. His breathing problem and his weight were a cause of distress for his parents. Such was the concern that this caused Ruby that she once lost her temper with Robert and stabbed him with a fork, an event that she and Robert remember well. Thankfully there was no malice intended and no lasting injury. Eventually doctors warned him he must lose weight and he was placed on a diet. Robert heeded the warning and gradually he lost his excess weight. Ruby was most proud of him on his wedding day when he was a slim and handsome bridegroom. However Robert's love of food has never left him and over the years his weight has increased, something which worries Ruby, and she wishes "He would go on a bloody diet today!"

More motoring misery for Frank and Ruby. In the early 1960s, Frank was working at the Tempered Rubber Company. One day his boss asked him if he would take one of the company's cars and drive down to Ford at Dagenham to deliver some urgently needed components. He decided that this would make a nice day trip for Ruby and Robert, then about three years old. Off they went and duly arrived at the factory, only to be told by the gatekeeper that there was no one around and that they should return at 10.00pm when the night shift would be at work. On their return they were met with disgruntled Ford men who complained that they had been waiting all day for the parts, and that there had been someone around earlier.

Setting off home, and being unsure of his way around London, Frank decided to follow a HGV vehicle, assuming that it would lead him to the M1 motorway, which it did. But just before getting on the motorway the car broke down. Frank went to a nearby phone box and called the AA, but no one arrived. Ruby, taking charge of the situation decided to call 999 and was put through to Scotland Yard, who assured her that someone would be with them soon, but no one arrived. She called them again, but no one arrived, and a third time. This time she was angry and told the police officer at Scotland Yard that she wouldn't come to London again even if the Queen herself invited her. Little did she known then that fifty years later the Queen would invite her.

Eventually a tow truck arrived and took them to a garage at Mill Hill, only to be told that the car could not be fixed and would take some days. Frank and Ruby were arguing with the garage man when a posh car arrived. The driver of the car heard the argument and offered to take Frank, Ruby and Robert, who fast asleep and quite oblivious to the predicament, into the centre of London, where they could be taken by the police to the railway station to catch the 4.00am train back to Sheffield. They arrived tired and exhausted in Sheffield at 9.00am. Frank's bosses were quite understanding, and they got the car back later in the week.

One Sunday Ruby was cooking the Sunday lunch and she and Frank were having a blazing row. Ruby reached boiling point and suddenly declared that she'd had enough and that she was leaving. With that she left the house and started walking away, not knowing where she was going. Shortly after she heard the sound of a bicycle approaching. She thought that Frank had sent one of the boys after her to get her to come back. Ruby told her son that she was not going back home, but the boy simply said "He doesn't want you back. He just wants to know how long the chicken's got to be in the oven."

In her younger days Ruby used to enjoy knitting and making woollen garments for the family. One day her mother told her that a new wool shop was opening at Gleadless Valley and so the two, with young Robert, set off to the shop to buy wool and a knitting pattern. To their surprise the shop was full, everyone being a member of the Sheffield United team. The shop had been bought by Joe Shaw, one of United's stars, for his wife and this day was the opening day. Ruby, it transpired, was the shop's first customer, and had her photograph taken with Joe and the team, the pictures appearing in the following Saturday's Green 'Un.

Back at home, United fan Gregory was in bed after his night shift. Ruby went in to wake him up and tell him that she had met Joe Shaw and shaken hands with him. Gregory told her "Don't wash that hand any more."

Weddings are full of excitement and expectations. Everyone wants everything to go without a hitch, but there's likely to be always something to cause a raised eyebrow or two. On the day of Graham's and Gillian's wedding things were going well up to entering the vestry for the signing of the registers. Ruby was resplendent in her outfit, including a fully feathered hat, the first of many hats for which Ruby has become legendary. However she made the mistake of leaning against a wall which, unfortunately, had a nail sticking out of it. When she moved the back of her dress was ripped in two and had to be hastily repaired with pins. The rest of the day was spent being careful not to move too much for fear of the pins coming loose and losing her dress. Nowadays the incident would have been caught on video and shown on "You've Been Framed" for all to laugh at.

The happy couple's favourite group The Whirlwinds played at the reception.

The 15th February 1971 was an important date in British history. That was the date when Britain changed its currency and went decimal. Out went the centuries' old pounds, shillings and pence (£sd), and in came pounds and new pence. Instead of twenty shillings, or 240 pennies to the pound, there were 100 new pence to the pound. Gone were the beloved ha'pennies, pennies, three penny bits, tanners, bobs, two bobs, half crowns and ten bob notes. Instead we got new half, one, two, five, ten and fifty pence pieces. The pound and twenty pence coins came in much later.

In Sheffield's shops and markets people were stood around looking at the prices on the stalls marked in the new currency units, and looking at the change in their hands, trying to make sense of it all. To add to the natural confusion, some old £sd coins were still valid as they had equivalent value to new decimal coins. It's no surprise that Ruby and her mother, like thousands of others, thought they were being robbed, especially as everything seemed dearer. It took some getting used to.

Some years after Frank's death, Ruby was living in a flat at Norfolk Park. Looking forward to a holiday in Spain, the day before her departure she fell into a hole and broke her leg. So, there was no holiday in Spain. But to make matters worse, three weeks later Ruby suffered a heart attack. She well remembers whilst in hospital being taken to have the plaster cast removed from her leg. But as she recalls, one good thing came of the calamity. She stopped smoking!

These days Ruby's photograph appears regularly in The Star, due to the 'Women of Steel' campaign, and she has appeared on TV. But her rise to fame started much earlier. One day she had gone to the Post Office to collect her pension and happened to see a notice asking for extras to appear in a film that was being shot on the Park Hill Flats. Ruby contacted the organisers and offered her assistance, along with that of Robert and Dawn. Arriving on set she was told to go to the make up tent, where she got talking to the other person in the chair next to hers, though she did not know at the time that the other chair was occupied by the film's leading actor, Keith Barron. She even asked him if she knew him, believing him to be someone she had once worked with. The would-be Hollywood 'A' Listers were well paid for their work, and well fed!

Kevin also joined them for one night and actually got a speaking part in the film. He was no stranger to acting, having appeared in school plays when at Hurlfield School. One play he was in, "Kes", was performed at Redcar in a schools drama competition, for which he was commended for his good acting. Redcar is now one of Ruby's favourite places to visit when she goes to stay at Kevin's and Lisa's caravan at Ugthorpe Lodge. The theatre where Kevin performed though has never been found.

Back to the filming, it was the practice for sets to be laid out at night ready for filming the next day. One evening a market set was set up, complete with stalls and goods on them. When people arrived the next morning to start, it was discovered that all the materials and goods on the stalls had been stolen.

It became a tradition in the Gascoigne family for Graham and Gillian to host the Vinnie Christmas Party named after Ruby's mother Lavinia. There would be a four course meal, and wine would flow, but family members had to arrive at the front door, and on time. The stairway in the house had a number of shelves, each of which held a brass ornament. At one party Lavinia got more than a bit tipsy, so much so that when needing the toilet she had to climb the stairs on her hands and knees. On reaching the top of the stairs she knocked a heavy brass horse off its shelf.

Unfortunately the horse landed on Brendan's wife Carole, causing her to suffer concussion.

Vinnie was not alone in her inebriated state, but the incident of the flying horse caused everyone to sober up quickly and attend to the injured Carole. When she recovered though she was subjected to the Gascoigne brand of humour and was the butt of many a joke such as 'feeling a little horse' and getting 'four faults'.

UNWANTED NEWS

In 1944 Ruby's father Ben was admitted to the City General Hospital, now part of the Northern General Hospital, for a hernia operation. She was allowed time off from her job at Flather's to go and see him in hospital, but noticed that he was looking gaunt. At home with her mother in the kitchen her mother suddenly said "Dad's shouting me" and then fainted. The day after a letter was received from the hospital informing them that Ben had died of peritonitis, strangely, at the time Ruby's mother shouted and fainted.

Ruby and Frank had lived for many years at Sky Edge. Here they had a happy life, but it was to be tragically cut short. They had not long returned from a holiday in Spain, a respite from looking after Ruby's mother, when on 2nd July 1984 Ruby and Frank were getting ready to go out in the morning. They were in no rush. Suddenly Frank started to complain that he was feeling quite ill, and was sweating heavily. He sat in a chair and died. The family doctor was called but Frank could not be saved. A heart attack had claimed his life.

By coincidence Robert had not gone to work that day and had gone to see the doctor, mumps being suspected. He was sat in the waiting room, unaware of the tragedy unfolding at his parents' home, when suddenly the doctor came rushing out of the consulting room and out of the surgery. Only later did Robert discover that the doctor was on his way to tend to Frank.

Ruby and her family, always very close to each other, were naturally grief stricken by this tragic event. The whole family rallied round their mother and gave her enormous support in this time of need. Frank was cremated at City Road Crematorium. Ruby did not tell her mother of Frank's death due to her condition and the fact that by now she did not know who Frank was.

The holiday they had just returned from, their last together, was not the usual kind of holiday they had previously enjoyed. Frank had been morose and complained of being cold. He had not joined in with many activities and had not been swimming in the sea, unusual for such a good swimmer. In hindsight Ruby wondered if this may have been a precursor to Frank's untimely death. Strangely, on this holiday, Frank spoke for the first time about his wartime experiences, of the deprivations he had suffered and witnessed, and of the friends and comrades he had seen killed.

Stranger still they had met a couple from Sheffield on the holiday, a mother and her daughter. The mother was a palmist and Ruby went to see her to have her fortune told. The woman closed Ruby's hand and told her to "Go back home and try and be happy."

Her son Graham decided that Ruby needed a break to take her mind off losing her husband. They spent a few days in Cornwall and it was whilst she was here that a second tragedy struck in the same month. Her eighty four year old mother died on 30th July, released from her totally debilitating and aggressive disease. She too was cremated at City Road. At the end of her days Ruby was a total stranger to her mother. She did not know her or know that she was married or had any children. A complete contrast to the active three times married woman she had once been.

All of Ruby's sons are, like their father was, staunch Sheffield United fans. A former United player, Freddy Furniss, was one of Frank's cousins. Bramall Lane was about the only place where Frank was ever known to swear. One match however, though not at the Lane, was never to be forgotten. The away night match was an FA Cup third round replay game against Burnley FC on Tuesday 12th January 1993. The brothers were travelling in two cars, Brendan and Gregory in the first, and Kevin and Robert with some friends in the second. The journey to Burnley was appalling with heavy snow falling and failed lights on the M62 motorway causing the motorway to be closed for some time. Traffic was slow and often at a standstill, but radio commentary kept the fans informed of what was happening on the pitch.

TRAGEDY

Everyone at Bramall Lane was stunned to learn of the death of Blades fanatic, Greg Gascoigne during the Burnley cup replay on Tuesday evening.

46 year old Greg, a Season Ticket holder for some 30 years, was caught up in the heavy traffic caused by the M62 closure and did not arrive at the ground until half time. He collapsed shortly afterwards and all attempts to revive him by the paramedics at Turf Moor failed.

He leaves a wife, Andrea, and three sons Dean, Lee and Mark, all of whom are true Blades as are his brothers Kevin, Brendan, Robert and Graham. We extend our deepest sympathy to them all and to the rest of Greg's family.

His dream was to see the Blades at Wembley so let us hope and pray that Dave and the boys can achieve that goal this season as a tribute to, and in memory of, Greg.

Gregory's death reported in the SUFC programme of 16th January 1993

All the boys usually travelled to away games together, but on this occasion Gregory was working a bit late, so Kevin and Robert set off earlier with some friends in order to get to Burnley in time for a pre match drink. Brendan left later with Gregory, and one of Gregory's work colleagues Tony Staley. When Kevin's party got to Huddersfield they hit bad traffic, with the M62 being closed by the police due to a lamp post having fallen onto the carriageway. They would be there for over four hours, and instead of watching United, they were having snowball fights. Having heard of the motorway closure, Gregory took an alternative route, but traffic here was very slow moving. They did however get to Turf Moor, Burnley's ground.

It was already half time when Brendan and Gregory arrived at the ground, and United were 3-0 up. They had just taken their places and were talking to people at the side of them when Gregory suddenly fell to the ground. He had suffered a heart attack which almost immediately took his life. St John's Ambulance men got him to the edge of the pitch but were unable to save him. His distraught brother Brendan, and his work mate Tony were in total shock and disbelief. Mobile phones in those days were not the popular items they are today so Brendan was unable to contact Kevin and Robert to let them know of the dreadful event. They in the meantime had found a gap in the motorway's central reservation and managed to turn their car round and were heading home, as the final whistle was blowing a Turf Moor, oblivious to their brother's unexpected and untimely death.

Ruby was babysitting for Robert's children when she received the phone call from a frantic Brendan to tell her the bad news. She then had to phone round to get hold of wives to inform them, and soon the family was gathering around Ruby and Gregory's wife Andrea. Later Kevin and Robert arrived to hear the distressing news. It was five o'clock in the morning when Brendan arrived home. Sheffield United won the match 4-2, but it was a most hollow victory. The next day the brothers returned to Burnley's ground to lay flowers on the spot where Gregory had died.

Gregory's funeral was adorned with many floral tributes including a Sheffield United shirt made of flowers from the brothers, and flowers from Burnley FC's directors. Ex United player Tony Currie and players from both the Sheffield United and Burnley teams, including Dave Whitehouse, Adrian Littlejohn and Burnley's goalkeeper attended the funeral. A football pitch made of flowers was also placed on Gregory's season ticket seat at Bramall Lane. In the following two matches when Sheffield United played at Burnley children in the family were team mascots.

United's FA Cup run ended when they were beaten 1-2 in the semi final by city rivals Sheffield Wednesday. Because of the status of this match it was held at Wembley, though the occasion was a sad one.

Not because of the final score, but because of Gregory's absence

Gregory's youngest child Jane had been born with a heart defect. Murmurs were discovered to be a hole in the heart, and at the age of two she had to undergo surgery to reverse her blood flow. She was coping very well after the operation but one Sunday, when she was five years old, she was at Frank and Ruby's house with her mother when she complained of hurting in her chest. The following day Frank took her to the Children's Hospital where it was discovered that Jane now had three holes in her heart and more surgery would be needed.

She had to undergo an eight hour operation, during which her blood flow was reversed again to its normal path. After the operation she had several tubes connected to her, but such was her recovery that most of these were soon removed. Unfortunately her blood clotted and, sadly, she died. She had been looking forward to starting school, but never got the opportunity.

Kevin's grandson, Jordan, is known to the family as the miracle boy. He too had a difficult time as a child. He has a condition known as Pulmonary Artesia with three ceptical defects which leaves many of his arteries to his heart and lungs not connected. He has undergone several operations, the biggest of which was in 2000. His surgeon on this occasion advised his family that such was his condition, he would only live for another 48 hours. But despite warnings that his life may be cut short, he has grown into a young man, amazing everyone in his family, who all love him dearly. He has battled against all the odds to work his way through school and studied photography at college. Among other things he has learned to drive, often chauffeuring Ruby about. Not content with all that, he is a charity fund raiser, raising money to buy wheelchairs for young people who suffer various illnesses that impair their mobility. Like his great grandmother Ruby, he has been featured several times in The Star. He is, says his grandfather

Kevin, "An inspiration to all his family and friends!"

Ruby is acutely aware that the present millennium has not been without its moments of great concern to both herself and her family. In 2000 Ruby underwent surgery for a knee replacement, followed two years later by that replacement being replaced. Her eldest son Graham suffered a massive heart attack necessitating an emergency operation. As a result he has had to retire early from his job as a master pattern maker, and reduce the distances of the walks he enjoys. Graham's wife, Gill, has also had a knee replacement.

Her daughter-in-law Lisa has suffered an embolism in one of her lungs, which required a stay in hospital, and she now has to have an injection before she takes a flight. Another daughter-in-law, Dawn, has suffered breast cancer and has a double mastectomy with several operations for reconstructive surgery. Dawn, a trained nurse, is now a champion supporting other women who are suffering the same devastating illness.

Throughout these anxious times Ruby has naturally found things very emotional, and has seen the stress and anxiety in other members of her family, their spouses and their children. She has spent many hours in hospitals as a patient and as a visitor. She has prayed for everyone to be all right and, as she happily says, "everyone came through it all."

HIGH DAYS AND HOLIDAYS

Since Frank and Ruby were re-united after he returned home from the war, the two and their young family had always taken a holiday. Frank was a hard worker and strove to ensure that his family enjoyed a decent life. He was a car owner at a time when cars were just becoming affordable to ordinary working men. The first holiday Frank and Ruby had abroad they took without their children. It was a time when holidays overseas was almost unknown for working class people, but Frank had served overseas during the war and so had an idea of what lay beyond the English Channel. To give the holiday an air of wartime romance, they flew in a converted patched up four engine bomber.

On their next holiday abroad they took their three boys and Ruby's mother. They had an early morning flight to France before taking a coach to Spain. They arrived at the airport early and were in for a shock, as airports in those days were not the kind of facilities they are today. Instead of a welcoming, all needs catered for passenger lounge, they were in a hut with no catering facilities, poor seating, and limited toilets. So early were they that they saw the plane they were due to catch go to France and return three times. At the Spanish border they had to change buses from a French one to a Spanish one, and currency restrictions at the time meant they could only each have ten pounds in English money with which to buy souvenirs, and for which they had to show proof of purchase when they arrived back in England. Their destination in Spain was Loret where, on one occasion, Ruby's mother got herself lost. When she was eventually found, she complained that no one could tell her where she was staying as they were all "bloody foreigners".

The owner of King Cole & Co, Charles Stamp, also ran a mineral water business called Aerosplash and Frank was employed as a part time salesman delivering drinks to local shops. Easter Monday in those days was always a popular time of the year. Not only was it a Bank Holiday, but an occasion for the Easter Parade, in which almost all the community took part. After parading through the streets those involved, and the followers, made their way to High Hazels Park at Darnall. Here there were stalls, games and refreshments, the latter being well supplied by Frank's deliveries.

Whitsuntide was the next festival in the Christian calendar and just as popular as the Easter Parade were the Whit sings. Choirs from many Church of England and Nonconformist churches would parade through the streets, with their respective bands, and all gather in a park, such as High Hazels, for a mass singing of hymns.

This was also the time when children received a new set of clothes, and it was traditional for the children to visit their relatives on Whit Sunday to show off their new attire. Relatives would give them a penny or two and doubtless tell them to look after their new clothes. Not that they would have much chance to enjoy them in those days, for the clothes were likely to be in the pawn shop soon after.

In 1966, the year of their Silver wedding anniversary, Ruby had been in hospital for an operation. To celebrate the anniversary Frank booked a touring holiday in Italy. They travelled down from Milan through the countryside and visited Rome, a place where Frank had been stationed in the war, and whilst here they took in the glories of St Peter's Basilica. In Naples they saw the United States fleet, and here Ruby was mistaken for a lady of the night.

The American sailors and their officers were ashore with three months' pay in their pockets. On an evening stroll Frank and Ruby were passing what appeared to be a small shop. In the window was an ornament which Ruby took a liking to. Frank said he would buy it for her and the two went inside. Frank went to the counter to ask its price whilst Ruby stayed near the door. It soon became apparent that the 'shop' was not a shop but something more seedy. An American naval officer then approached Ruby and asked her if ten dollars would be enough. The shop was a brothel and an indignant Ruby put the sailor in his place. Frank succeeded in buying the ornament, which Ruby still has, and the shop, they discovered, was owned by one of Al Capone's henchmen!

Continuing their journey they came to Pompeii and after making their tour of the site, Ruby fell into a hole and required first aid. It turned out that the hole was part of a German archaeologist's excavations. The tour included a trip to the Isle of Capri, home of the English singer and actress Gracie Fields. For five pounds tourists could take tea with Our Gracie, but Frank and Ruby decided five quid each was too much for a cuppa, and gave it a miss. The holiday ended with a trip to the Blue Lagoon and a journey by boat into the caves.

Not all holidays took them abroad and after their third son was born they found that Butlin's at Skegness was a great place for an enjoyable family holiday. The food was good and fun was to be had everywhere. At the time they used to go to Butlin's some unknown, but later to be famous entertainers, performed there, people such as Irish comedian Dave Allen who was a redcoat, and Beatles drummer Ringo Starr played in the band there. There was always a competition to enter such as knobbly knees and beautiful baby, and Ruby's mother Vinnie won the Grandest Grandmother competition.

The services available at Butlin's included a crèche and a night nurse service who kept an ear open for any crying babies, whilst parents were at one of the bars or theatre. A crying baby would be reported on a blackboard and the show's compere would announce that a baby was crying in chalet 'X'. If it was Frank and Ruby's chalet, invariably Frank would go and see to his weeping son.

Later holidays by air and by road took the family to several countries, though with the older two children now grown up and holidaying with their friends, the family holiday included Frank, Ruby, Brendan, Kevin and Robert.

In later years Ruby has travelled alone on holidays, but usually with the same travel company. Places visited include Austria, France, Spain, Croatia, Germany, Majorca, Ireland and the United States, where they visited their old friends Viktor and Irene Gruza in Florida, the last time in 1981. Ruby reckons she's done the Dover-Calais crossing about forty times. These holidays in far flung places all a far cry from the days of a 2s 6d (12½p) trip by char-a-banc (coach to modern readers) to the seaside.

1977 was the Queen's Silver Jubilee year and Frank and Ruby holidayed in Bulgaria with their youngest son Robert. One evening in a restaurant there was no table immediately available but another party of four, two men and their wives, were sat at a large table and were happy for the Gascoignes to join them at their table. During the course of the evening the two parties got talking to each other and it was mentioned that Ruby's eldest son, Graham, was a master pattern maker who had served an articled apprenticeship at the English Steel Corporation's River Don Works in Sheffield, but had had to leave when the company became part of the nationalised British Steel Corporation. He was now working at Steel & Garland in Worksop. One of the other men, a foundry manager in Halesowen, was surprised to learn this and disclosed that all the patterns used in his foundry were in fact made by Graham. Small world!

By the time of Frank's death, their next holiday in Spain had already been booked for September. They were to go with her son Gregory and his wife Andrea. Andrea's mother agreed to fill Frank's place on the holiday, and all was set when out of the blue the holiday company, Shelmar, went bust, and worse, there would be no compensation. Kevin and Robert contacted both The Star and Yorkshire TV's Calendar to highlight the dilemma, and Ruby was seen on that evening's programme looking sad and unpacking her suitcase.

Later that evening Gregory and Andrea received a phone call from another tour operator, Siesta, saying that they were willing to take the group to Spain for the cost only of the coach fare. For £18 each they enjoyed a fortnight in Salou in a brand new unused apartment which the company was going to offer in its next season's brochure. Ruby wrote to the company to thank them for stepping in at the last minute, and has travelled with them many times since. She became one of their regulars, on first name terms with the coach drivers.

Ruby was never a lover of flying and always had to take some medication with her to prevent air sickness. She would be worried about flying before the holiday started, and again before travelling back. Since Frank's death though she doesn't fly anymore, despite many protests from her sons. She prefers to travel by road and sea. This means a three day journey, with an overnight stay in a Madrid hotel, before and after a visit to her son Brendan's house in Spain. The rest of the family enjoy having holidays at Brendan's Spanish retreat, where he intends to retire to in due course.

After Frank died Ruby started to cook Christmas dinner for all the family. But she then moved to a flat which was too small to accommodate the Gascoigne clan, so the occasion relocated to Kevin's and Lisa's house, a tradition which continues. For a party in excess of twenty, Kevin cooks a four course meal, complete with champagne, served on tables which he hires, with chairs, especially for the occasion. In the evening the rest of the family arrives for a party with plenty of fun and games. Guests bring sleeping bags, but Robert and Dawn have their own special blow up double bed and duvet. The following morning Kevin is to be found again at the cooker, preparing a full English breakfast, and in the afternoon the boys set off for the Sheffield United Boxing Day match.

On 16th October 2011 Ruby and her 'Women of Steel' colleague Kathleen Roberts were guests of honour at Bramall Lane for the United v Wednesday derby match. After brunch with United's directors, they were introduced to the teams and led them out onto the pitch where they were introduced to the fans. They won the day! The teams though could only manage a 0-0 draw.

WOMAN OF STEEL

The Second World War broke out on 3rd September 1939, and, as in the First World War, many of Sheffield's women were called upon to do jobs previously undertaken by men who had now been called up for active service. This meant jobs in the steelworks, engineering and munitions factories, and many of the firms that supplied these industries.

"When you got to 17 you had to register for the Forces – the Land Army – you went virtually where you were told – including into the steel works... There were women then who were crane driving but during the War they did just about everything including some of the heavy jobs. They used to work shifts like the men."

For some it was the first job they had ever had. For others it was quite different from anything they had done before. For most, it was conscription, under the terms of The Registration of Employment Order 1941. Doing nothing without good reason was not an option. Thousands of women were employed in jobs far removed from the noisy and dirty environment of the steel works and similar places of work. Even in those factories women were conscripted into office and canteen work, as they were into food production, sales work and other jobs that kept the country going in these days of war when life "just carried on."

It was quite common for women to drive cranes and locomotives, to operate drop hammers or lathes and milling machines, to work on furnaces, to weld, and any number of lighter jobs. At the end of it all, there were no thanks for the sterling work they had done. Even at the

"I speak to you all alike, men and women...The lives of our sons and brothers, our own future as free men and women, and the peace and civilisation of the whole world, depend on the effort we make now to produce arms and win the war...You have worked hard and steadfastly – work harder still...give of your very utmost..."
Words of wartime Minister of Supply, Herbert Morrison MP

end of the First World War some firms, like the National Projectile Factory at its Templeborough Works (operated on their behalf by Thomas Firth & Sons), gave their women workers a card declaring "An Appreciation of loyal services...", but not at the end of this conflict!

The women doing these jobs were numbered in their thousands. They accounted for one fifth of Hadfield's 10,500 employees and about half of Metropolitan Vickers 2,500 strong workforce. Other large employers such as the English Steel Corporation, Firth Brown's, Edgar Allen's and Brown Bayleys would have employed women in similar numbers. The proportion of women workers would have been around the same in smaller, but no less important, factories producing steel products, components and munitions.

No one knows for sure how many women were employed in this type of war work. Very few of the hundreds of Sheffield firms that produced materials for the war effort, including many whose traditional output was not militarily related, now exist. But an indication of the number of women working in these factories can be gauged by the fact that, despite them being paid less wages than their male counterparts, the wage bills trebled.

After the war most women returned to the chores of being a wife and mother, though many continued in paid work of one sort or another. The jobs they had been doing for the war effort were now taken up by those men who had returned from Europe, the Far East, the Royal Air Force and the Royal and Merchant Navies, and who were needed to rebuild a shattered Sheffield. The women *"had done what needed doing and thought nothing else of it."* [Women of Steel]. There were no thanks!

Rightly the soldiers, sailors and airmen who fought for freedom, both the dead and the survivors, are remembered in several memorials. In recent years there have been successful campaigns to get the work and roles of other groups of people, whose efforts were no less significant in the war, recognised and honoured. The women of the Land Army for instance now have full recognition. But the women of Sheffield who filled the men's work boots have never been so honoured – until now.

It was former wartime steelworks employee Kathleen Roberts who in November 2009 wrote to The Star to ask the question why women like her had never been formally recognised for their efforts. The Star's Nancy Fielder took up the gauntlet and asked for other women to write in with their stories of the parts they played and the jobs they did. There were hundreds of replies from women like Kathleen, all of them octogenarians and nonagenarians, including one from Ruby, one of the first received, though only after her daughter-in-law Dawn had her urged to write in. Dawn later contacted Nancy Fielder, who then came to interview Ruby and take photographs.

"I am so pleased that people are just beginning to realise what we went through because this is history and when we have gone, what we did has vanished.

"I don't think anybody really knows what we were really doing in the steel works. We did our share during the war and sometimes probably a greater share but nobody had even thought about doing something about this."

Kathleen Roberts

Later that month Richard Caborn, then Labour MP for Sheffield Central, who was fully behind the campaign, made arrangements for some of the Women of Steel to go to London to put their case for recognition of their wartime work to Kevan Jones MP, Parliamentary Under Secretary of State & Minister for Veterans. They would also meet other local MPs and visit Downing Street.

On 13th January 2010 Ruby and Kathleen Roberts, and two other local wartime women steel workers, Kit Sollitt and Dorothy Slingsby, set off by train, first class of course, for London to meet Britain's top political leaders. As an additional tribute East Midlands Trains named the train that ferried them to London 'Women of Steel', and they were treated to a champagne reception. Their outfits for this special day were provided courtesy of Atkinson's store, and their hair styled by hairdressers Headlines Elite.

> *"That this House recognises the enormous contribution to the war effort made by the Women of Steel who played such a valuable role in the Second World War carrying out crucial jobs in South Yorkshire's steel and engineering industries producing vital parts for planes, tanks and bullets; welcomes four representatives of the Women of Steel to Parliament on 13 January; notes they are to meet the Minister for Veterans and to visit No 10 Downing Street; and hopes that as a result of this campaign led by The Star newspaper the Government will formally recognise their contribution at a national level."*
>
> House of Commons Early Day Motion 12th January 2010

The Women of Steel campaign attracted the support of other Sheffield MPs – Nick Clegg (Lib Dem, Hallam), Meg Munn (Lab, Heeley), Clive Betts (Lab, Attercliffe), David Blunkett (Lab, Brightside) and Angela Smith (Lab, Hillsborough). On the day before the visit to London the local MPs had submitted an Early Day Motion in the House of Commons, to get the campaign officially recognised by the government.

The visit to London included calling at the Ministry of Defence where the women received a formal thank you from Kevan Jones MP, lunch at the House of Commons, followed by a meeting and tea with Prime Minister Gordon Brown MP at No 10 Downing Street, with whom they shared a few jokes about their steel works days.

Kit Sollitt even reminded the Prime Minister that workers paid extra income tax during the war, and enjoyed spending it when it was repaid many years later. *"Nice and cuddly"* was their opinion of Mr Brown. They also met Alistair Darling MP, Chancellor of the Exchequer. Ruby later received a hand written note from the Chancellor and his wife saying *"Dear Ruby, Thank you for visiting us here at No 11. With our very best wishes, Maggie and Alistair."* Their visit made national news with both the BBC and ITN giving it mention, as well as national newspapers.

In March came a letter from the Ministry of Defence putting the Ministry's, and the nation's, formal thanks in writing for the contributions and sacrifices made by Ruby and the thousands of Sheffield and South Yorkshire women like her. The letter pointed out that *"Britain was the only country to conscript women as well as men"* in the Second World War.

MPs said :

"It has been absolutely fantastic, a real recognition for the contribution that many hundreds, if not thousands of women did during the war years." Richard Caborn

"It is a great occasion and a really lovely way to say thanks, not just to these women but to those who are no longer with us." David Blunkett

"I think it is really nice for us in Sheffield to recognise that actually it was women who were doing the jobs that most of us thought of as men's jobs." Meg Munn

"I know that the women are really, really grateful for the recognition that they have received but it is their due." Angela Smith

"We are giving publicity and a bit of stardom to people who at the time thought 'I'm just doing my job'. Clive Betts.

This was followed by an invitation to the Holiday Inn Royal Victoria Hotel in Sheffield where Ruby and her colleagues received personal recognition for their efforts by Kevan Jones.

In April the Women of Steel received Sheffield's own thanks at a civic reception in Sheffield's Town Hall hosted by local MPs and civic leaders. Ruby was one of almost 200 wartime women workers who attended the reception, and were entertained to a concert of wartime songs sung by children from Arbourthorne School. In fact two receptions had to be arranged to safely accommodate the number of women keen to attend, some meeting old wartime work mates for the first time since 1945.

Each of the attendees received a certificate from the Lord Mayor, Councillor Graham Oxley, who said *"These women were heroic, strong and gave of themselves for others' benefit. I am proud on behalf of the city to be here with them to mark Sheffield's official thanks for what they did for us. They contributed in no small part to the victory over Hitler and to the freedom we all enjoy today."* He told the women guests *"We are extremely proud of you in Sheffield for the work you did in the wartime years and the effort you made towards victory in 1945. You had no choice but you didn't make a fuss about that, you just knuckled down and got on with the jobs in those strange, dirty and difficult conditions at a time when we had our backs to the wall."*

Councillor Paul Scriven, then Liberal Democrat Leader of Sheffield City Council, said *"It has taken far too long to celebrate with you the work that you did but it is a great day of pride for all of us in Sheffield."* Labour Group Leader, the late Jan Wilson, added *"The amount of living history in this room is amazing."*

Their stories have also been captured for posterity in mediums other than The Star's Women of Steel campaign, and their accompanying *'Women of Steel'* book.

Students at the University of Sheffield's School of English interviewed Ruby, Kit, Dorothy and Kathleen for a film they were making as part of the Storying Sheffield project. In the interview comparisons were drawn between the wartime lives of these women and those of today's young women. The point was made that the lives of Ruby and her friends was dramatically changed the day war was declared. Ruby recalled that her wartime life was determined by work, bed, tram timetables and her young son. A Women of Steel DVD was released in 2011.

Along the way during the Women of Steel campaign, Ruby and her colleagues were in almost constant demand giving interviews to groups of students, and on radio and television. Ruby appeared on BBC Radio 4's *'Woman's Hour'* programme…

In March 2010 she gave a recorded interview of her experiences which as been has lodged with the Second World War Experience Centre in Leeds. She was in Leeds again where she was interviewed and filmed at Real Life Media Productions. Later, in November, she was invited to a photographic session at the Magna Adventure Science Centre near Rotherham. The Centre was formerly part of the giant Steel, Peech & Tozer steel works, part of the United Steel Companies, where many of the Women of Steel would have spent their wartime working days and nights. This event was organised by Emma Ailes for her *'Britannia'* book and exhibition.

In March 2011 Ruby and her friends were present at the University of Sheffield's Women of Steel event where they were invited to give their personal recollections to students following the showing of a film that had been made by a recently deceased student. Guests and students *"saluted the amazing vigour"* with which Ruby spoke.

More national recognition came when the Women's Engineering Society held its annual conference in Sheffield in November 2010. The women were invited to the Society's conference to speak to members, and then to the Gala Dinner at the Cutlers' Hall. *"It seemed an unmissable opportunity for WES members to meet with and celebrate the achievements of these women who come from the generation that inspired the founding of our society."* wrote Dianne Patterson in the summer 2011 edition of the Society's journal. She interviewed six of the over 200 women who had responded to The Star's campaign, including Ruby, and added *"...they had many things in common, for example, joy in their memories and in their life...".* To top this off the women were made honorary members of the Society.

CROWNING GLORY

The quest for recognition of the Women of Steel's work did not end at Downing Street, for Ruby's son Kevin wrote to Her Majesty the Queen.

I am writing to draw your attention to a campaign that has been taking place in our local evening newspaper, the Sheffield Star. The campaign has been running over the last few months, to try and gain recognition for the Yorkshire ladies, or girls as they were then, that kept the steelworks running during the Second World War, under the title of "Women of Steel".

My mother, Ruby Gascoigne, is one of these ladies, and today they are taking their campaign down to London, as they have been invited to the Houses of Parliament, and to Downing Street. As I have said, my mum was merely a girl when she was forced to take a job at Flather's steelworks in Sheffield back in 1939.

All the men folk that normally ran the works were being called up to fight for our country, but it was essential that the steelworks were kept running, as they made the parts for tanks, aircraft, bombs etc.

The work was hard, but these girls did all that was asked of them, often handling top secret materials, and producing very important metals, vital to the war effort. I have worked in the steelworks myself, and even today the work is hard and certainly not suitable employment for young girls. At least I was able to go home and relax after a hard day's work, these girls ended up going down into bomb shelters, or clearing up the mess left by the devastation that was caused in Sheffield.

My mum got married, but didn't see her new husband for 4 years, as he was serving his country. She had to live through the trauma of my father's parents being killed in the Sheffield blitz, but still they continued to keep the steel mills rolling. At the end of it all, they never received so much as a thank you.

They had done every bit as much as the Land Army girls or the brave men that fought, but their work was never deemed worthy of thanks or reward, although to be fair, they never asked for any thanks, they saw it as their duty.

We all love to listen to my mum's stories, but none of us can ever really imagine what people went through during those awful times. Without these heroes telling us what happened, we would never really know what people went through for all of us. I find it really hard to take when a sportsman gets an OBE or an MBE for their services to sport, or when an actor gets rewarded for services to acting. These people have done absolutely nothing compared to the wonderful things done by people of my mother's generation, and I feel that it is still not too late to let them know that the country is grateful for what they did.

I am not asking for OBEs or MBEs for these women, deserved as they would be, but I feel that Her Majesty would love the opportunity to tell these ladies herself that their work was appreciated. My mum has always been very much a Royalist, and I know that just a few moments spent with our Queen would be the pinnacle of her very worthwhile life.

Would it be possible for these ladies to have the opportunity to visit the Palace? Time is running out for most of the girls, and I feel that my generation owes them all so much, and I personally would go to any length to ensure that when my mum dies, she will know that she did everything she possibly could do for her country and her family, and that her work was appreciated by us all. This campaign has given her a new lease of life, and I have just waved off the 4 ladies, as they boarded their specially named train on their way to London. Please Ma'am, could you try and set aside a few moments of your very busy schedule, just to say a personal than you to our Women of Steel. It would mean so much to them all.

I have the honour to be, Ma'am, Your Majesty's humble and obedient servant.

Kevin Gascoigne

The letter did not go unnoticed. The Royal eyes had gazed upon Kevin's words and a response was despatched stating *"Her Majesty has taken careful note of your comments regarding those women who worked in the steel industry during World War II, when all the men were called up to fight. I must tell you however that this is not a matter in which The Queen would personally intervene, nevertheless, I have been instructed to forward this letter to the Garden Party Office in the Lord Chamberlain's Office."* However nothing came of this, so Kevin decided to write again, this time to HRH Princess Anne the Princess Royal, having previously met her at a corporate function. This time the letter resulted in an invitation to Ruby, himself and another Woman of Steel to attend a Royal Garden Party

In preparation for the big event Ruby had to acquire for herself a new outfit, one suitable for a Buckingham Palace summer Garden Party – and a hat of course. In this she was afforded the services of a Marks & Spencer personal shopper at Meadowhall, together with a contribution towards its cost. A cream tea was also included in the luxury shopping trip.

The day started with free first class rail travel to London, and after checking in at their hotel, the Union Jack Club, the party had a light lunch before walking the short distance to Buckingham Palace, though it was not quite such an easy walk for Ruby as for the others. They were ushered through a few of the Palace's rooms before entering the gardens. Here Ruby took a seat in one of the marquees, just as well, for the heavens opened and it rained for the rest of the afternoon. Kevin, Kathleen and her daughter wandered around and saw several royals, including HM The Queen, HRH the Duke of Edinburgh, HRH Prince Charles and the Duchess of Cornwall, HRH Princess Anne and HRH the Earl and Countess of Wessex. But Ruby remained dry in the marquee.

Ruby really enjoyed the evening, guest of producer Bill Kenwright at the London Palladium, where Michael Crawford was appearing in 'The Wizard of Oz'. This was another event originated by Ruby's son Kevin. Having written to Bill Kenwright (who used to appear in Coronation Street as Betty Turpin's son Gordon) to inform him of the Women of Steel campaign, and the part played by Ruby, and of the invitation to the Garden Party, he asked if they could round the day off with an attendance at one of Mr Kenwright's productions. The response was immediate and positive, seats at the London Palladium and arrangement to meet the leading actor and actress.

The party were met by their own personal uniformed usher who, after Ruby and Kathleen had availed themselves of the private Ladies' Room, were shown to their seats, the best seats in the house. Their drinks were waiting for them on a reserved table at the interval, and after the show the party were taken back stage to meet Michael Crawford. The leading lady, Danielle Hope, unfortunately was not in the cast on this evening.

Ruby says that when Michael Crawford had finished removing his make up and came to meet them, he appeared as though he was a long lost friend and Ruby and the party got on very well with him. She mentioned that she had seen him in 'The Phantom of the Opera' at the Sheffield Arena and, as she points out, could have stayed chatting with him all night. The party had taken with them a copy of 'Women of Steel' to give to Michael and Danielle Hope, which he warmly accepted with thanks.

The following morning the party made their way to the Imperial War Museum, again the journey taking its toll on Ruby, but Kevin had gone ahead and when Ruby got there, a wheelchair was waiting for her. They were, according to Ruby, treated like royalty, and met several of the Museum's directors and senior staff and were given a full guided tour. They had a number of photographs taken and a copy of 'Women of Steel' was given to the Museum. From there the party made their way back to the station for the first class journey home.

Kathleen Roberts and Ruby are greeted at Bramall Lane by ex United and England star Tony Currie

In true goal scoring fashion, Ruby waves to the United fans

On their way to No 10 Downing Street: left to right: Kathleen Roberts, Kit Sollitt, Dorothy Slingsby and Ruby

These ladies are not for turning!

And at the heart of government.
Ruby and her fellow travellers
in No 10 with former Sheffield
Central MP Richard Caborn, and
Prime Minister Gordon Brown MP

A guardsman has to look his best
when posing for the camera with
two special visitors

Ruby with Michael Crawford in his dressing room at the London Palladium

Ruby, Kit Sollitt and Dorothy Slingsby at the plaque unveiling ceremony, 5th November 2011

Sheffield City Council Leader Cllr Julie Dore and Lord Mayor Cllr Sylvia Dunkley address the crowd at the plaque unveiling ceremony

The Women of Steel plaque

Ruby in a festive mood
with her five sons

Ruby with her family at the christening of her great, great granddaughter, Ruby.

STATUE

As a contribution to the Women of Steel campaign, plans were put forward in February 2009 by Sheffield City Council to erect in the city a permanent memorial to the women workers who played such a vital role in the city's steel works and munitions factories, and associated firms, during the Second World War. Richard Caborn MP said *"I think it is part of our heritage, something Sheffield feels very proud of, and to put that as a permanent reminder is something I would fully support."* Councillor Graham Oxley, then Sheffield's Lord Mayor, told women guests at the civic reception in Sheffield Town Hall in April *"It will be a permanent reminder of your work and of course, those who are no longer with us. You will be remembered forever with that statue. That is a great honour because even royalty and ex Prime Ministers don't get a monument until they are no longer with us."* The idea also formed part of a formal motion put to the City Council in March 2101.

> *"...believes that there should be a permanent monument to the 'Women of Steel' in a prominent city centre location in Sheffield... therefore requests the Chief Executive report back to the Cabinet within two months on proposals to ensure the Council can ensure this goes ahead."*
> Extract from the motion to Sheffield City Council 3rd March 2010

The City Council set aside £28,000 as the basis of a fund to pay for the memorial, and asked local businesses to contribute to the estimated £150,000 cost of the project. Barker's Pool was chosen as the preferred site of the memorial, being the site of the city's War Memorial. But a year, and a change of civic administration later, nothing had happened.

As late as August 2011 though there was a promise from City Council Leader Julie Dore of a plaque being sited in Barker's

Pool as an interim measure, prior to the commissioning of a full memorial from a noted sculptor.

Ruby said in The Star "It is about having a statue there after we have gone and for those who have already gone. We are not getting any younger and we would love to see the statue finished. We didn't work for thanks but now we know what we did was vital to the war. We released a lot of men to go into the forces to fight. My whole family, as well as hundreds of other families, feels very strongly that nobody really appreciated what Sheffield women did before The Star's campaign. My life was ruined working 13 hour nights, coming home to see my baby and then spending the rest of the time in the air raid shelter while my husband was away, for four years."

The project took a step forward when on 5th November 2011 a plaque commemorating the Women of Steel was unveiled in Barker's Pool, by the City Hall. Ruby, Kathleen Roberts, Kit Sollitt and Dorothy Slingsby were in attendance, along with many other former Women of Steel, and their families to hear City Council Leader Councillor Julie Dore and Lord Mayor Councillor Sylvia Dunkley praise and acknowledge the work done by Sheffield women in both World Wars. Also in attendance were Pam Liversidge and Suzanne Liversidge, respectively the first woman Master Cutler and first woman President of Sheffield Chamber of Commerce & Industry, and a future Woman of Steel Amy Pryce, an apprentice with the Sheffield forgings firm Firth Rixon. The ceremony was followed by a Tea Dance in the Winter Gardens.

On 8th February 2012 the City Council announced that the services of renowned sculptor Martin Jennings had been secured to produce the planned permanent memorial to be sited in the city centre. Noted for, amongst other works, his statue of poet Sir John Betjeman at London's St Pancras Station, his design for the sculpture was deemed to be the best and most appropriate of all the candidates' proposals. Ruby was fully involved in the selection process, and Martin consulted the Women of Steel to help him formulate his design.

He commented "It's a great honour to have been asked to make this important monument in Sheffield." Ruby said "We all agreed Martin was the perfect candidate for this project. His work is wonderful, he knows how to tell a story through people." It is anticipated that the memorial statue will be unveiled towards the end of 2012. A fitting tribute to all the Women of Steel of both world wars, and a lasting legacy of women like Ruby.

FINAL THOUGHTS

Moments before her husband Frank died, he put his arms around her and told her "You'll never know how much I've loved you." Having come to terms with his sudden loss, Ruby realised how close the two of them had been. She lost not only her husband and lover, but her best friend. The two of them had done a lot together, and with their sons. It was her sons who rallied round her in her time of need, as indeed they did only a few years later when her second son Gregory suddenly died.

Reflecting on her childhood and the bond between her and her parents, her closeness to her aunts and uncles and cousins, her marriage, her sons and their families, and taking into account all that has happened in the good times and bad times, Ruby makes one thing quite clear – her life has been, as she herself has put it, "truly blessed."

BIBLIOGRAPHY

Stand House School 60th Anniversary 1st October 1931 – 91
Manor Memories Group, 1991
The Blitz 50th Anniversary December 1990
Manor Memories Group, 1990
The Tinsley Chronicle
Stephen Johnson, 2010
The Woman Engineer, Summer 2011
Women's Engineering Society
Women of Steel
Nancy Fielder, 2010

Ruby Gascoigne (front row, far right) and colleagues from
W. T. Flather's Standard Steel Works in World War Two